# PERCEIVING OTHERS

The psychology of
interpersonal perception

MARK COOK

# PERCEIVING OTHERS

The psychology of interpersonal perception

METHUEN
LONDON AND NEW YORK

First published in 1979 by
Methuen & Co. Ltd
11 New Fetter Lane, London EC4P 4EE

Published in the USA by
Methuen & Co.
in association with Methuen, Inc.
733 Third Avenue, New York, NY 10017

Typeset by Inforum Ltd, Portsmouth
Printed in Great Britain at the
University Press, Cambridge

ISBN 0 416 71550 8 (hardback edition)
ISBN 0 416 71560 5 (paperback edition)

*British Library Cataloguing in Publication Data*

Cook, Mark
  Perceiving others.
  1. Social perception
  1. Title
  153.7'5      HM132

# CONTENTS

158·2
C772b

252155

# PREFACE

This book is intended as a short introduction to the area of social psychology variously called 'person perception', 'social perception', or 'impression formation'. These rather clumsy names effectively conceal the fact that it is a very interesting topic – the way people see each other, the way they interpret each others' moods, predict each others' behaviour, and sum up each others' characters. The way people see each other determines the way they behave towards each other, so the study of 'person perception' is one of the keys to understanding social behaviour.

Research on these topics started over one hundred years ago, with Darwin's book on *The Expression of Emotion in Man and Animals*, and has flourished, with ups and downs, ever since. It would be impossible even in a very massive book to review every single experiment or even every theory; a medium length introduction has to be very selective indeed. Material has been included if it interests me, or if it appears to interest a lot of my colleagues working on person perception; current or recent trends in research such as attribution theory or the impression formation paradigms are fully covered.

To save space I have referred to literature reviews, where they exist, rather than to every individual experiment.

This book started life as a title – *Interpersonal Perception* – in the Penguin Science of Behaviour series, although I doubt if there is much of the 1971 version left recognizable after two major revisions. I am very grateful to Methuen for giving me the chance to re-write and up-date it. The major changes are the inclusions of two new chapters, on attribution theory and combining multiple cues, a condensing of the section on accuracy and a general up-dating and re-writing, in what I hope is more readable and interesting English.

I would like to thank my colleagues and students at Oxford and Swansea for ideas, inspirations and references they have given me, Robert McHenry, Michael Argyle and two anonymous reviewers for comments on the manuscript, and my wife for her patience while I have been occupied writing and re-writing this book.

M.C.

# 1 THE PROBLEM
## Issues in person perception

> I do not love thee, Dr Fell
> The reason why I cannot tell
> But this alone I know full well,
> I do not love thee, Dr Fell
>
> Thomas Brown, 1663–1704

Most people don't often stop to ask themselves about the opinions they form about other people, about how and why they form them, nor about their correctness. They choose their friends without knowing why; they trust some people and not others, but can't say why; they ask one girl for a date and not another for no apparent reason; they get married in blissful ignorance of what their partners are really like. Paradoxically the opposite often happens too; people form opinions about others, assert them dogmatically, and allow them to determine their whole attitude toward another. How often do people form an 'instant dislike'? Or insist, in the face of mounting evidence to the contrary, that someone is entirely trustworthy? Forming opinions about other people can be a profession; in as short a space of time as five minutes, the interviewer decides on a person's suitability for employment, promotion or admission to higher education, and thereby affects that person's life for years to come. Many interviewers have a well-developed sense of their own infallibility, coupled with a near total lack of insight into how they reach their verdicts.

The purpose of this book is to cast a critical eye over the way people perceive each other, a field of research traditionally given the rather clumsy and not entirely appropriate name 'person perception'. Seeing someone drop a hammer for the third time and saying 'clumsy' to oneself goes quite a bit beyond the usual meaning of 'perception'. 'Person cognition' would be a better name, if it did not sound so pretentious.

For those who like definitions, person perception may be defined as the forming of judgements about other people, particularly those that concern people as social animals. However, the word 'judgement' is a little misleading because it suggests a careful, conscious weighing of the evidence, awareness of making a judgement, and awareness of what the judgement is; very often people would be unable to report all, or even any, of these three things. A better definition of person perception might take the form: 'the ways people react and respond to others, in thought, feeling and action.'

This chapter will start by considering what sorts of things people say, think and feel about each other, to give some idea of the phenomena to be explained, and will then outline what appear to be the main issues and questions that have arisen.

## Varieties of person perception

DIFFERING TIME SCALES

> Our visitor bore every mark of being an average common-place British tradesman, obese, pompous and slow . . . there was nothing remarkable about the man save his blazing red hair and the expression of extreme chagrin and discontent upon his features.
>
> Dr Watson's thoughts in
> *The Red-Headed League* by
> Sir Arthur Conan Doyle

Many personal traits – sex, age, personality, intelligence, social class, mental and physical abilities – don't alter much from day to day; others change on a time scale of weeks, days or hours. For example, moods, and the facial expressions that reveal them, usually last only a few hours, or even minutes, whereas the desire to continue speaking, and the cues by which the speaker conveys it, can change from second to second. Very few things about people never vary; even sex can be surgically altered. Enduring/changeable is a dimension in terms of real time scales, but tends to be a dichotomy for the perceiver. People are often surprised when they find that someone has visibly aged or got a new job, but not if his good temper has turned to bad.

The list of words for describing people's moods or emotions is very long; some of those intensively studied by psychologists are: 'anger, fear, happiness, disgust, contempt and pain.' Many of these words are metaphorical or refer to the cause rather than the expression. What is the difference in terms of facial expression between embarrassment, chagrin, and shame? Probably not much – the difference lies elsewhere, in what caused the expression, or the observer's opinion of its worthiness. Research has tended to look at expressed emotions in isolation, overlooking what or who caused the mood; compare 'he is angry' with 'he is angry with Jones [not me] because Jones contradicted him'. Other changes cannot really be called moods or emotions, but are indications of the person's attitude to what someone else has said or to what the person himself is saying. Liberman (1965) took some account of the complexities of real life when he studied tone of voice in a bored statement, a confidential communication, an objective question, a pompous statement, and expressing disbelief and doubt.

SUPERFICIAL AND DEEP DESCRIPTIONS

> Mary is a girl friend back [home]. We went to school together for one year. She is about 5'6" and has red hair. She's a lot of fun. She has a real good sense of humour; she's fun to be with . . . She's real smart . . .
>
> [Ruth] dates fairly much but she can't seem to go toward one boy and when she does like one boy she sort of falls hard and then if the boy doesn't like her as much as she likes him, she has a real rough time . . . She's worried all the time that a boy is going to drop her . . . She's sort of insecure . . .
>
> Two US College girls describing their<br>best friends, from Secord and Backman (1964)

Many observations about other people are superficial: nationality, race, social class, occupation, age and physical appearance. Such observations aren't particularly important in themselves, except that they often determine initial impressions and elicit stereotypes. Vernon (1964) points out that stereotypes based on superficial acquaintance can be very useful: 'social intercourse would become chaotic if we did not straight away react differently to a sixty year old and a six year old, to a society hostess and a prostitute.'

Superficiality, like changeability, is a dimension rather than a dichotomy. An assessment of specific behaviour like 'he always slams the door' or 'he plays football well' goes deeper than mention of appearance, age or occupation, while a description of personality itself, expressed in such terms as 'he is ill-mannered/sadistic/good at music', goes still deeper. Accounting for people's behaviour – 'he drives very fast because he is aggressive' – gives the appearance, if not always the actuality, of even deeper insight. Appropriately 'depth psychology' offers the most profound, or profound-looking, accounts of behaviour. A proposition like 'he is ill-mannered because he is basically insecure and trying to boost his self-confidence' not only describes the person's behaviour, but explains it by reference to the interplay of processes below the surface of behaviour or, in the Freudian accounts, below the level of consciousness. Many critics have pointed out how hard it is to ascertain the truth of such statements.

Pseudo-profundity is of course the stock-in-trade of fortune-tellers, astrologers and some psychologists. An experiment by Snyder and Larson (1972) has shown how easily convinced most people are by a seemingly deep analysis of an individual's character. The same set of platitudes, e.g. 'disciplined and controlled on the outside, you tend to be worrisome and insecure on the inside', was given to every student in a class, and most accepted it as a genuine and profound interpretation of their own personality. The experimenters dubbed this the 'Barnum effect', after the American circus proprietor who coined the phrase 'there's one [sucker] born every minute'. Secord's unpublished study, described in Secord and Backman (1964), suggested the 'depth' of description of another's personality may itself be a consistent personality difference. Some college students described friends in simple terms like 'good at dancing, fun to be with' whereas others offered elaborate psycho-dynamic accounts of people's inner conflicts and complexes. This sort of investigation – other examples of which are discussed in Chapter 6 – suffers from the problem that subjects in psychology experiments tend to think profound psychological interpretations are what the experimenter wants, rather than the seemingly trivial and mundane things the subject actually thinks.

PERSONALITY TRAIT NAMES

abandoned          given up to vice, extremely wicked or
                          sinning without restraint, irreclaimably
                          wicked, as in *an abandoned villain*.

zoophilous         animal-loving.

(The first and last words in Allport
and Odbert's (1936) list of 17,953
trait names, as defined by Webster's
*New International Dictionary*)

'He will not be able to give me the correct change' is a very specific prediction, whereas 'he is bad at figures' is more general, and 'he is not very intelligent' is about as general a statement as one could make. Words like 'intelligent', that say something about a whole range of behaviour, are called 'trait words'. Some apply to a relatively limited area of behaviour – 'fatherly' or 'ill-mannered' – whereas others cover the whole of a person's thoughts and actions – 'extrovert' or 'quick-witted'. There are an enormous number of trait words in the English language – Allport and Odbert's (1936) famous analysis, using Webster's *New International Dictionary*, listed nearly 18,000, some admittedly archaic, metaphorical or of marginal relevance. Psychologists have not been slow to add more to the list, and many have become popular terms, e.g. 'inferiority complex', 'high need for achievement' or 'cyclothymic'.

*The logical status of traits*
The philosopher Gilbert Ryle (1949) pointed out that trait words are 'dispositional terms'; a dispositional statement like 'glass is brittle' or 'Jones is stupid' tells you what glass or Jones have done in the past, and are likely to do in the future, e.g. break if struck, give the wrong answer if asked a simple question. A trait word *summarizes past behaviour* and *predicts future behaviour*. The relationship between a trait statement and statements about particular events is often complicated. The statement 'Jones is intelligent' covers an enormous range of behaviour, from his skill at verbal reasoning to his taste in reading, but doesn't definitely imply any particular item. The statements 'Jones is intelligent' and 'Jones can't play chess' aren't contradictory; intelligent people are not perfectly and exhaustively consistent in their intelligence. The same is much more true of personality traits; soci-

able people are not invariably and on every occasion, sociable. Hence an exception to a dispositional statement about personality or intelligence doesn't disprove it anymore than a single consistent example definitely proves it. (Curiously enough it has been shown recently that the ability to characterize someone's personality, in trait terms, and the ability to predict what will happen on a particular occasion are separate, and to some extent opposed (Fancher, 1967). The *better* someone is at 'summing someone up' in a character sketch that others could use to identify the person described, the *worse* he is at translating this summary into a statement about what will actually happen on a particular occasion.)

*The empirical status of traits*
People are fairly consistently intelligent across different tasks, as Spearman first discovered; that is why it is possible to talk about 'general ability'. The same is not true for many personality traits, where exceptions to the rule are often so numerous as to make the rule useless as a tool for predicting behaviour. The classic example is honesty, studied extensively in Hartshorne and May's (1928) 'Character Education Inquiry'. Hartshorne and May had the idea that 'character' – traits of honesty and persistence – could be measured like intelligence, and the tests used to select and train pupils. This proved impossible because the intercorrelations between the thirty or so tests used were uniformly very low. Not merely was there no correlation between tests of honesty in reporting money 'found' and tests of honesty in reporting athletic achievement, but even trivial variations in procedure resulted in tests failing to correlate, so that the tendency to crib from one answer book didn't predict the tendency to crib from another. Similar results have been reported for other traits, such as dependency, conditionability, aggressiveness, and attitude to authority; the evidence is reviewed by Mischel (1968).

*The usefulness of trait descriptions*
Hartshorne and May's findings imply that it is meaningless to say someone is honest unless the circumstances are specified. (Thus a character reference mentioning a shop assistant's honesty would probably be taken as meaning honesty in handling money.) However, confusion arises when the person hearing an unqualified trait statement thinks it means one thing, while the person who made it meant something different. Oldfield (1939) asked

a number of psychologists what they understood by 'reliability' and found that some thought it meant predictability – always doing the same thing – while others included the notion of consistently meeting obligations – always doing the *right* thing. Others again defined it more specifically, taking it to mean the ability to work without supervision, or even to mean refraining from saying things one would later regret. Given that the link between a trait description of someone and their actual behaviour is often so tenuous, it is not surprising to find that trait words are not always useful information. Rodin (1972) found they were much less useful as aids to identification than descriptions of specific characteristic behaviour, such as 'apt to keep you talking for hours'. Trait descriptions were however more use than metaphorical descriptions; being told someone was 'like a possum' was no help at all in identifying them.

TRAITS AS EVALUATION

> Mavole's father must be that midget with the eyeglasses
> like milkbottle bottoms who enjoyed sweating so much.
> Richard Condon, *The Manchurian Candidate*

If something doesn't really exist – and Hartshorne and May's data seem to show that honesty doesn't exist as a consistent behaviour pattern – why is there a word for it? Allport and Odbert (1936) argued that because trait words are part of the language they must have some meaning. The argument that there must be an actual something if there is a name for it is obviously false – consider unicorns – but it is strange that there should be so many trait words in the English language, and that they should be so widely used, if in fact there is nothing being named. Some traits are 'real'; there is a consistent pattern of behaviour corresponding to the word 'intelligent'. Others, such as honesty, describe patterns of ideal rather than actual behaviour. A great many more, such as 'nice', 'kind', or 'likeable', mean that the speaker approves of the person described, without implying anything specific about his behaviour – in psychological jargon, they express positive evaluation. This is well-illustrated by the line from Condon's *The Manchurian Candidate*. The description of Mavole's father tells the reader little about him, except that he is small in stature and myopic; it says by contrast quite a lot about the character thinking it – that he doesn't like small people, nor short-sighted people, nor, probably, people in general, and that he has an irrational paranoid belief that people sweat deliberately, in order to annoy him.

## Mischel's view of traits

Mischel (1968) suggests that many traits exist in the mind of the perceiver, rather than in the behaviour of the perceived; he goes on to suggest, rather indirectly, that their primary function is to *impose order* on the flood of information about other people's behaviour, rather than to *detect an order* actually present. It would be impossible to remember or communicate all the thoughts, utterances, and actions of every person one knew, so in order to remember what one thinks of them and to tell other people what one thinks, one resorts to the oversimplification and frequent distortions of trait language.

Mischel is wise to be less than explicit in this suggestion because hard evidence is lacking. He points out that people can only discriminate about seven (seven *plus or minus two*) levels of volume, brightness, or pitch, so that it is reasonable to suppose that people's ability to distinguish different personalities might also be severely limited. In fact, even seven *minus two* is an overestimate; Bieri *et al.* (1966) showed that some people can only distinguish two levels of maturity or aggressiveness in others. A study by Dornbusch *et al.* (1965) shows that a person's choice of trait words is idiosyncratic; it is easier to predict who will use a particular term to describe others, than it is to predict who it will be used to describe. Would one get the same results if ten people each described a house or a car? Or would they all use the obvious dimensions of size, colour and price, so that one would know which house or car was being described, but not who was giving the description? Houses and cars are simple, compared with people, so descriptions of them would reflect their true nature, not the observer's need to feel he understands them. Mischel could also cite the voluminous literature on stereotypes, discussed in greater detail in Chapter 4, which shows that people do indeed oversimplify their judgements of other people, often to the point of absurdity.

## Conclusion — the status of trait descriptions

Person perception depends on trait descriptions quite heavily; the reply to the question 'What is he like?' is very likely to include at least one trait word. Such trait words are just as likely to say something about the person using them as about the person being described, and will probably reveal whether the user likes or approves of the person he is describing. When the trait name isn't largely evaluative, it may point to an ideal pattern of behaviour, such as honesty, or to a notional one, such as conformity; when it points to real patterns of behaviour, such as intelligence, the link between the trait and concrete behaviour is complex and indeterminate. These properties of trait descriptions affect the sort of question the researcher can sensibly ask about them.


PERSONAL RELATIONSHIPS

> 'Diana hates Jack?' – 'That's what she said' – 'You mean she had to tell you? The first time we met them Diana couldn't bear Jack, and she's gone on not being able to bear him ever since. How funny you've never noticed.'
> Adapted from Kingsley Amis, *The Green Man*

Claims about personality traits are difficult to verify, but observations about like and dislike aren't. The statement 'Jones doesn't like Smith' can be checked very easily by asking Jones; unless one has grounds for supposing Jones is lying, there is no sensible way of contradicting him – he couldn't possibly be mistaken. The study of like and dislike in groups was pioneered by Moreno, who called it 'sociometry'; Tagiuri (1958) in turn introduced the phrase 'relational analysis' to describe experiments on perception of like and dislike in groups of people. Relations between people, like their moods, can be a lot more complicated than the simple case of 'I think Jones doesn't like me'. Consider, for example: 'Jones perceives that Smith knows that Brown doesn't like Smith although Brown thinks Smith thinks Brown does like Smith.' This seems impossibly obscure written down, but describes an everyday phenomenon, for which the term 'impression-management' has been coined. Every person is trying to create a particular impression on the people he meets – often different impressions on different people – and is naturally keen to know whether he has succeeded or not. Since there is a taboo on commenting on the process of impression–management (Goffman, 1956), it's very hard ever to be sure what effect the performance has. It could reasonably be said that research on the perception of personal relationships has not generally, with the occasional exception, come to grips with the complexity of its subject.

THE VARIETIES OF PERSON PERCEPTION – CONCLUSION

It is possible to characterize the way people see each other in terms of a number of reasonably straightforward dimensions and categories – long/short time scale, superficiality/profundity, evaluative/descriptive, perception of emotion, personality, ability, personal relationships – so as to give some idea of the scope of the subject. Such an analysis also points to the fact that apparently simple propositions – he is an intelligent, honest, likeable reliable person – contain a variety of surprising complexities and need to be analysed on different levels. Research on person perception can be criticized for sometimes failing to allow for the complexity of its subject matter and studying things at too simple a level, preferring the misleading simplicity of 'he is angry' or 'Jones likes Smith' to the confusion of the ways people actually talk and think.

## The issues in person perception

A   Jones is a nice, kind, considerate person.

B   Jones will fail in medical school, because he doesn't work very hard and isn't very bright.

The sort of questions that can be asked about the first description of Jones are very different from those posed by the second. Of statement A, one can ask about the structure of impressions – do the terms 'nice, kind and considerate' usually go together? One can ask what sort of person makes positive evaluations about people readily, and how they will affect specific predictions about Jones's behaviour. One can ask what Jones has to do to be judged as nice, kind and considerate, and how other circumstances affect the impression he makes, and conversely what would lead to Jones being judged as 'nasty, unkind and inconsiderate'. The one question that can't sensibly be asked is whether the judgement of Jones's niceness and kindness is correct.

Of statement B, one can ask whether the prediction that Jones will fail is correct, and whether the assertions that he is not very intelligent and doesn't work very hard are true. One can ask what sort of person makes accurate predictions about others, and whether this ability can be learned, or improved by training.

Of both statements one can ask how the person deals with more than one item of information – 'nice, kind, considerate', or 'doesn't work very hard and isn't very bright' – in reaching an assessment and particularly how he manages when these items are inconsistent – 'nice, kind and inconsiderate' or 'doesn't work very hard but very bright'.

Very broadly speaking, three questions can be asked about the way people form opinions about others – what are the processes involved, what information is used and how, and how accurate are they?

The most important problem for the psychologist is how judgements of others are formed: Chapter 2 outlines two different types of explanation of the judgement process. It also considers whether the same model will account for judgements about enduring characteristics, like personality traits, and for perception of rapidly changing states, such as interest in what is being said. Chapter 2 limits itself largely to opinions based on one item of information; the expert, if not always the layman, uses a variety of information, which poses the question, discussed in Chapter 3, of how the information is used, especially when it points in different directions.

The second principal issue in person perception – what information is used and how – is discussed in the next three chapters. Chapter 4 starts with the more superficial information conveyed by non-verbal behaviour, such as facial expression, and by race, occupation, age or appearance – the 'stereotype'. Chapter 5 considers the way people interpret more substantial sequences of behaviour, within the framework of 'attribution theory' which seeks to explain in particular the way actions are interpreted as evidence of personality. Chapter 6 completes this section by considering the way personality traits are seen as going together, and how value judgements nearly always enter into one's impressions.

The third issue – whether judgements are correct or not – is discussed in the last three chapters. Chapter 7 analyses the surprisingly complex methodological and statistical problems this apparently simple question poses. Chapter 8 reviews the evidence on how good people are at seeing each other accurately, and what makes a 'good judge of others'. Chapter 9 considers specifically the accuracy with which 'professional person perceivers' – personnel selectors and psychiatrists – reach their conclusions.

# PART I
# PROCESSES INVOLVED IN PERCEIVING OTHER PEOPLE

The layman is more likely to be interested in the correctness of the opinions he forms of others or in the information he uses to form them – topics discussed in Parts II and III – while the psychologist is primarily interested in how the judgements are formed. He argues that only by knowing how something is done, can one understand why it is done well or badly.

Research on person perception has been carried out in a wide variety of traditions, and that on the processes involved is no exception. It starts in a philosophical vein, considering the way in which knowledge about other people may be acquired, moves into a more clinical tradition, in considering the inference model of perception, and then shifts slightly, while remaining in the clinical area, into a consideration of different mathematical models.

The earlier work on intuition and inference accounts of person perception, which is described in Chapter 2, tended to confine itself to perceptions formed on the basis of a single piece of information, whereas later research, described in Chapter 3, tries to take account of the more complicated, but more typical case of basing a perception on a number of pieces of information.

# 2 INFERENCE OR INTUITION?

## The mechanisms of person perception

'As to your practice, if a gentleman walks into my rooms smelling of iodoform, with a black mark of nitrate of silver upon his right forefinger, and a bulge on the side of his top hat to show where he has secreted his stethoscope, I must be dull indeed if I do not pronounce him to be an active member of the medical profession.'

Spoken by Sherlock Holmes, in
*A Scandal in Bohemia* by
Sir Arthur Conan Doyle

The main issue in the history of models of the way people perceive each other has been: is perception of others inferential or intuitive? Do people form opinions in the conscious, analytical, step-by-step fashion of Sherlock Holmes? Or, do people 'just know' what they think about others, in a way which, if it isn't extra-sensory perception, is unanalysable and unconscious? Women in particular have been credited with the power of 'just knowing' – women's intuition – but many other groups of people – doctors, social workers, personnel officers, even some psychologists – flatter themselves that they have the mysterious gift of intuition.

## Intuition models of person perception

Webster's *New International Dictionary* defines 'intuition' as: 'knowledge obtained, or the power of knowing, without recourse to inference or reasoning; innate or instinctive knowledge; insight; familiarity; a quick or ready insight or apprehension.' This definition contains several different notions, and, in fact, intuition theories of person perception put forward at least five different propositions.

## PERCEPTION IS INNATE

Thomas Reid (1764) said, 'Nature is so constituted that certain empirical facts are signs of certain metaphysical facts and human nature is so constituted as to be able to interpret these signs intuitively.' 'Natural signs' include facial expressions and gestures.

Reid is arguing that the expression of some emotions, as well as their recognition, relies on innate mechanisms. Darwin (1872) is of the same opinion and also considers emotional states to have evolved from adaptive responses; for example, in the expression of disgust the nostrils pucker up, to exclude the unpleasant smell, and the mouth moves as if to spit out something nasty. There is some evidence that expression of emotion can be innately determined in men and animals. In animals most expressive behaviour is instinctive – dogs do not have to learn to growl when threatened nor to roll over on their backs to submit. Ethologists argue that animals instinctively recognize things about other animals – by the so-called innate-releasing-mechanisms – but most of their examples are taken from birds, fish or insects (Tinbergen, 1953). Sackett (1965) has shown that monkeys reared in isolation respond appropriately to the facial expressions of monkeys; since these responses couldn't have been learned, this is evidence for instinctive recognition of emotions in animals. More recently Comfort (1971) has argued that sexual interest in humans may, as in animals, be communicated by sexual odours or 'pheromones', response to which is innate; however, while there is good evidence for the role of pheromones in animals, and especially in some species of insects, the evidence for human pheromones is sketchy and unconvincing.

It is much more difficult to show that either expression or recognition of emotional states in humans depends on instinct; children cannot be reared in isolation to study the effects. Ekman (1972) has tackled the problem in two ways; he has established that simple emotions are expressed facially in the same way in a wide variety of cultures including the USA, Brazil, Chile, Argentina and Japan. He has also shown that children born blind show recognizable facial expressions. Normal children might learn to express things facially by watching others, or by looking in a mirror, but blind children obviously could not. However, as the blind children grow up, their expressions remain limited in number, and crude and indifferentiated in character.

It is much more difficult to find evidence that people recognize facial expressions instinctively. Ekman's work has shown that New Guinea tribesmen could make reasonably good sense of European facial expressions, although they had never seen white faces, nor their expressions, previously; however, given that the tribesmens' own facial expressions were reasonably like those of Europeans, this is not proof of instinctive recognition.

The expression of emotional states in humans, as in animals, partly depends on innate mechanisms; it is possible, but not definitely proven, that human recognition of emotion may also be partly innate. There is no evidence that other sorts of judgement depend on innate abilities; indeed it is obvious that the majority of them must be learned, for it is inconceivable that much, if any, of the machinery for making judgements about suitability for medical school, or about tendency to suicide, could be inbuilt. People must somehow learn to reach conclusions like these about each other.

PERCEPTION IS GLOBAL

The Verstehen ('understanding') school of psychologists (Spranger, 1928) stated that people understand others by 'an act of intuition encompassing their personality as a whole'. For example, the reason for a dislike of dogs might differ radically in different people, in one man reflecting merely a painful encounter with a dog in childhood, in another reflecting a distrust of blind obedience and loyalty. The dislike of dogs in turn throws light on another aspect of the men's behaviour, and forms part of each man's unique configuration of attributes. The argument that 'the whole is greater than the sum of the parts' has been well-aired of late in the 'clinical and actuarial assessment' controversy, which is discussed in detail in Chapter 3. Gestalt psychologists also emphasize the global aspect of perception by suggesting that people, like objects, are perceived as meaningful wholes. There is ample evidence that impressions are organized in meaningful ways, that people assume associations between different characteristics and that discrepant information is ignored or distorted (see Chapters 3 and 6), but it is also clear that people can give judgements on isolated aspects of personality, sometimes from isolated items of information; perception is not *necessarily* global. Cattell (1937) attacked the Verstehen school and the argument that people can only be understood as meaningful wholes, as obscurantist and unscientific, contributing 'nothing except a magic word, the purpose of which is to cry "Halt" to the irreverence of further investigation of personality'. He considered the proper role of psychologists was to analyse global judgements, not to sit back and admire them.

## PERCEPTION IS 'IMMEDIATE' OR 'DIRECT'

The distinction between 'direct' and 'indirect' perception, or between 'immediate' or 'mediated' perception, looms large in the history of philosophical thought about intuition. It was supposed that certain types of knowledge, for example the distinction between right and wrong, or the fact that $2 + 2 = 4$, were known in a special way, by a special faculty called intuition. (For detailed discussion of this philosophical background, see Westcott (1968) or Sarbin, Taft and Bailey (1960).) Arguing that people form impressions about each other by some such special faculty tends to remove the topic from the scope of scientific psychology; it is another example of a 'magic word', to use Cattell's phrase.

However, philosophy has changed its character over the last 40 years, and now looks with intense suspicion at the notion of special knowledge and special faculties for obtaining it. The philosopher Austin (1962) pointed out that, in the context of perception, ' "directly" takes whatever sense it has from the contrast with its opposite'. Unless one is contrasting 'direct' perception of people with some specified form of 'indirect' perception – hearing evidence, seeing someone in a film – it is meaningless to talk of 'direct' perception. It gives the appearance of drawing a profound distinction but it is in fact merely misleading.

In the context of person perception there are two theories that offer some explanation of the distinction between 'direct' and 'indirect' perception: the Gestalt theory of 'isomorphism' and 'empathy' theory.

### Isomorphism

The Gestalt theory of person perception, outlined by Arnheim (1949), relies on the concept of 'isomorphism'. 'Isomorphism' is derived from Greek and means 'same' (iso) 'shape' (morphism). According to

Arnheim, one person perceives another person's mood through a series of isomorphisms. The 'psychic structure' of the person's mood is reflected in an 'isomorphic' pattern of physiological forces, which in turn produce an 'isomorphic' pattern of facial expression and posture. This is perceived by the observer and translated back into an 'isomorphic' psychic structure in the observer, who thereby perceives the other's mood.

This is not a satisfactory explanation of how facial expressions are perceived, but rather a series of misleading metaphors and false analogies. What is 'psychic structure' and how is it determined? In what sense can the pattern of physiological forces have a shape and how could such a shape match the physical dimensions and angles of the facial expression and posture? And doesn't the theory imply that the observer will share the other person's mood, rather than perceive it? Arnheim's account fails to explain the distinction between direct and indirect perception.

*Empathy*
Empathy theory states that the perceiver knows what the other is feeling, because he imagines himself in similar circumstances, or has actually had the same experience himself, so that when the perceiver sees what is happening to the other person, he experiences the same emotion himself. For example the man who winces when he sees a work mate drop a brick on his foot is showing empathy.

Stotland (1969), who defined empathy as experiencing an emotional reaction as a result of perceiving another experiencing an emotional reaction, produces evidence that empathy can occur, although he comments on a lack of consistency in the results. All his research deals with reactions of fear and pain: it is less certain that people would react with actual feelings of pleasure to the sight of something nice happening to someone else. The anxiety produced by painful or frightening experiences is known to generalize readily to anything even remotely connected to the original event, which would obviously tend to include the sight of someone else about to suffer the same. Not all perception of emotion depends on empathy, for people can perfectly well see another's mood or emotion without sharing it. (Experiments on how well people can predict each others' answers to personality tests are sometimes called 'empathy' studies, which is misleading because neither emotion nor feeling the same as the target feels need come into it.)

## PERCEPTION IS INFALLIBLE

'Direct' or 'intuitive' perceptions are sometimes also thought to be infallible. Systems of philosophy often use as their starting points propositions, intuitively derived, that must be true, which can serve as sound bases from which to derive further inferences. Evidence reviewed in Chapters 7 and 8 speedily dismisses the suggestion that judgements about other people are necessarily always correct; they are often systematically biased and sometimes totally false. Being convinced that a belief or judgement is true is in any case no guarantee that it is correct. The accuracy of opinions about others has been repeatedly shown to be unrelated to the confidence with which they are held (Oskamp, 1962).

## PERCEPTION IS INSTANTANEOUS OR VERY RAPID

A fifth meaning sometimes implicit in intuition theories, or in accounts of 'direct' perception, is that perception is very fast – so fast that the idea of any intervening perceptual processes seems absurd. Allport (1937) is very impressed by this argument, and suggests that the reader can impress him or herself equally by a simple demonstration: 'While riding in a public conveyance close your eyes and turn your head toward some fellow passenger . . . open your eyes for a brief glimpse lasting two or three seconds and then with your eyes closed introspect upon the impressions as they arise.' Impressions of 'sex, age, size, nationality, profession, and social caste' will be followed by impressions of his 'temperament, past suffering, his "hardness", his ascendance, friendliness, neatness and even his trustworthiness and integrity.'

Allport cites one or two early experiments on the speed with which opinions of others can be formed, including one by Engelmann (1928) that employed thirty-second interviews. Allport's argument fails however to impress contemporary psychologists, who know that perception is a rapid process, as well as a complicated one, and who don't think that the perceiver has any privileged information about his own perceptual processes. Yet while perception is rapid, it is not instantaneous; Morin *et al.* (1965) found that it took people on average 0.61 secs to recognize and name a friend, which suggests that the two or three seconds recommended for Allport's demonstration may be longer than necessary. Given that people often argue from similarity of appearance to similarity of personality it isn't surprising that a glance at a stranger is enough to evoke a large number of impressions. Nevertheless, Allport's demonstration points to the continuing neglect of research into the time scale of judgements of personality and emotion. An unpublished study by Cook and Smith has shown that it takes an average 0.53 secs to recognize simple emotional expressions, and studies of psychiatric diagnosis and selection interviewing, reviewed in Chapter 9, find that the psychiatrist or interviewer often reaches a verdict within the first five minutes of the interview. But, on the whole, not enough is known about the time scale of person perception.

CONCLUSIONS

Intuition accounts of person perception contain as many as five different propositions which for the most part are not logically related. For example, the speed with which an opinion is formed is logically unrelated to its correctness, dependence on instinctive mechanisms, or specificity. Similarly, an opinion formed by the operation of innate mechanisms – supposing such occur in humans – might equally be global or specific, although the ethological data on instinct in animals generally describe highly specific responses to highly specific signals.

All the propositions of the intuition approach have a degree of truth, albeit a very limited one in the case of 'direct' perception (and it is arguable that data like Stotland's can be more simply explained in terms of learning motivated by fear). The degree of truth of two of the propositions – that perception is 'direct' and that it is innate – probably applies only to the recognition of emotional states. Another proposition – that perception is global – is true of many judgements, but is not a necessary feature of perception.

The claim that perception is 'direct' – the most important feature of intuition theory – is meaningless unless the nature of 'indirect' perception can be specified; no convincing account of the distinction has yet been offered.

## Inference models of person perception

Inference models of person perception deny that impressions of others somehow arrive fully formed in the mind, and argue instead that they are formed in the way Sherlock Holmes habitually employed to impress Dr Watson: 'Men with stethoscopes are usually doctors. This man has a stethoscope. So he is probably a doctor.' The combination of previous experience – doctors use stethoscopes – and present information – he has a stethoscope in his hat – forms the opinion.

The best known account of person perception in specifically inferential terms was developed by Sarbin *et al.* (1960). Simplifying their elaborate account considerably, the observation that a man is aggressive divides into three stages, approximating a classical syllogism:

> All red-haired men are aggressive
> This man has red hair
> Therefore he is aggressive

The first line is a generalization about a class of people. The second notes that the generalization applies to a particular person and the third draws the inference. The generalizations in the first line of the syllogism have been called 'postulates', 'schemata', 'constructs', 'inference rules' and 'implicit personality theories'. Inference theory is not strictly speaking a theory, rather an explanatory model using an analogy with symbolic logic. It provides a useful framework for studying person perception but does not generate any testable predictions.

PROBLEMS WITH THE INFERENCE MODEL

No psychologist could take seriously the claim that the way people understand other people is fundamentally unanalysable, for, as Cattell pointed out, it is the business of psychology to provide such an analysis, but the name given to theories that seek to provide the analysis – 'inference' – is unfortunate. Guiora (1965) points out that 'inference' implies a slow, deliberate step-wise process, in which the perceiver knows the premises, is aware of making a deduction from them, and can say what the conclusion drawn is – precisely all the things perception generally does not involve, at least for people who do not have a mind like Sherlock Holmes. Meehl (1961) argues forcefully that perceptual processes may not be formally inferential like Sarbin *et al.*'s model, and that it is an error to confound an account of how perception *might* work or *ought* to work, with an account of how it *does* work.

Psychologists are fond of seizing on analogies to explain human behaviour – the brain is like a computer, anger is like water under pressure in a pipe, person perception is like the formal logic of the classical syllogism. The first two analogies are very misleading; Meehl thinks the third probably is too. Inference accounts of person perception should perhaps assert no more than that there is an analysable perceptual process involved.

## The role of consciousness

It is sometimes argued that when forming impressions of others, people are not aware of going through the three stages of inference, for they do not approach social encounters as if they were a combination of a detective seeking clues and a logician drawing inferences. (This is an irrelevant objection and harks back to the time when psychology relied on introspective evidence.) Ask a non-psychologist how he knows that one thing is further away than another, and he is unlikely to be able to talk about retinal accommodation, stereoscopic vision, perceptual constancies or the like. One infers distance from mundane cues, such as superimposition – an object in front of another is closer – or known size, or from less obvious cues such as texture gradients – the further away something is, the fainter and greyer its colour. Similarly most interviewers would strenuously deny that they worked on such an irrational basis as supposing that men who wear glasses are more intelligent, or that women who wear lipstick are frivolous but it is very easy to demonstrate the existence of either stereotype by asking interviewers to assess persons presented with or without either accessory.

One reason the perceiver does not know how he operates is that perception is very fast, but this fact which so impressed Allport is common to all perception of familiar material, and to all skilled performances. In fact, Bruner (1957) and Westcott (1968) both suggest that what people call intuitive perception is really perception where the conclusions are reached without conscious consideration of the steps involved, and where the process is skilled and well-practised.

## Meehl's criticism — inference or regression?

A more serious objection is made by Meehl (1961), who considers it a grave error to confuse a 'causal analysis' and a 'logical reconstruction' of person perception. He also objects that the syllogistic analogy imposes categorical thinking on the model, which is misleading. The major premise of many syllogisms starts by saying 'all men', but this is something the psychologist can never do, for no interesting generalization about human behaviour is invariably true. In practice 'all', in generalizations about behaviour, usually means 'nearly all' or 'most' or very often merely 'some'; but this undermines the inference model, for nothing follows logically from the major premise 'Some X are Y' and the minor premise 'This X is Y'. One can never draw valid syllogistic inferences about human behaviour, because the major premise is never absolute. Of course, perceivers often do draw fallacious inferences about 'all people' from major premises about 'some people'; arguably this is what prejudice is all about.

Meehl (1961) suggests that a model based on the concept of correlation is a more fruitful analogy, avoiding misleading all or none, categorical thinking. The perceiver knows the probability of one attribute going with another – the *redder* someone's hair, the *more aggressive* he is *likely* to be. The perceiver does not think in terms of categories but in terms of dimensions and the relationships between dimensions. The relationship between *redness of hair* and *aggressiveness* is expressed mathematically by a correlation coefficient. A high positive correlation would mean red hair goes with aggressiveness; a high negative correlation would mean red hair in fact went with meekness; a low or zero correlation would mean that hair colour says little or nothing about personality.

The correlation model is particularly suited to describe judgements based on a number of cues, not just one. In formal judgements like psychiatric diagnosis – the focus of Meehl's interest – the judge always has more than one cue, often dozens. To express a syllogistic inference from ten not necessarily consistent cues, would be very clumsy. Does one have a separate major premise for every possible combination of ten cues? In which case one would need hundreds of different major premises, each on the lines of 'People who have eyebrows that meet in the middle, whose hands shake, who talk about wild dreams they have, but who do not have criminal records, are fairly dangerous'. Or does one draw ten separate inferences each for a single cue, then somehow combine them? In Meehl's correlation model by contrast, the contribution of 4, 10 or even 20 separate items to predicting dangerousness could be summed up in a one line 'regression equation'. This gives a numerical value to each piece of information, to the extent that it reliably predicts 'dangerousness'. Items that do not predict much get a low value, while items that do predict 'dangerousness', but add only information already contained in earlier items, also get a low value.

However, experiments on the perception of imperfectly correlated variables throw some doubt on Meehl's analysis. For example, Gray, Barnes and Wilkins (1965) gave college women sets of paired values of two abstract qualities, X and Y. In different conditions, the value of Y was closely correlated (0.96), moderately correlated (0.78) or poorly correlated (0.44) with the value of X. After seeing a sufficient number of pairs to become acquainted with the size of the correlation in their condition, the women were given the value of X alone and asked to predict Y. In the high correlation condition the women's task was of course simple, since there was virtually a one-to-one relation between X and Y – if X is 9, then Y is also likely to be 9. However, in the conditions of moderate and poor correlation the correct strategy would be to allow predictions of Y to 'regress to the mean', that is for X = 9, tend to choose values of Y nearer 5 (on a nine-point scale). The logic is easier to follow from a scatter plot of items measured on two dimensions that correlate poorly, c. 0.40, and relatively highly, c. 0.90. Such plots can be found in many statistics texts. For a low correlation, like 0.44, most of the points form a loose ellipse in the centre of the diagram, so that even for an extreme value of X, the bulk of corresponding Y values do not differ much from the average. Only when the correlation is very high does an extreme value of X imply a high probability of a similar value of Y. The women did not however follow this correct strategy, but tended still to assume a one-to-one relationship, even in the poor correlation condition. They seemed unable to grasp, or at least use, the concept of two things being related, but only to a moderate extent.

A similar study, using less abstract material, has been reported by Kahneman and Tversky (1973). They employed personality sketches, which served as the subjects' basis for predicting what post-graduate courses a student would enrol in. As in Gray *et al*.'s study the correlations between the sketch and the course prediction was varied – by the simple expedient of telling half the subjects the sketch was a good predictor, the other half that it was a poor one. Kahneman and Tversky's study differed however in one respect: subjects were also given a simple list of the proportion of students enrolling in different post-graduate specialities, which showed that Arts and Humanities attracted, or at least admitted, more than twice as many students as Computer Science. It follows that if one had to make a guess about a student's future course choice, knowing nothing about him, then guessing that he will do Humanities is more likely to be right than guessing he will do Computer Science. Similarly if one has to make a prediction from information said to be unreliable, so that one is not far off guessing, the same strategy is best. In fact, subjects largely ignored both the information that the personality sketch was unreliable and that some courses had far larger numbers of students; if the sketch seemed to indicate Computer Science – that was what the student was expected to do.

The tendency of people to use information that 'looks good' even when it is actually unhelpful or even useless is most strikingly documented in a study by Chapman and Chapman (1967). They presented subjects with a series of responses to the Rorschach ink blot test, paired with statements about the people who did the test, e.g. is homosexual. Some of the Rorschach responses were valid cues to homosexuality, e.g. seeing the blot as part man, part animal, others were not valid, but looked plausible, e.g. a person's backside. In Chapman and Chapman's study the responses and the symptoms were randomly paired, regardless of the true validity of the response. After a series of such trials, the subjects were tested to see what they had 'learned' about Rorschach responses. They should of course have 'learned' that the Rorschach responses were completely uninformative. In fact, they 'learned' that the plausible but invalid signs were indicative of homosexuality. Chapman and Chapman's subjects were in good company, that of the clinical psychologists and psychiatrists who first generated the popular, plausible, but invalid theories about the meaning of the Rorschach. In subsequent studies Chapman and Chapman found that people still clung to the plausible, invalid signs, and would not use the valid ones, even when the pairings in the 'training' series were altered to reflect the true validity of the cues. This study shows that people do not always learn from experience what goes with what, but rather select cases to fit a pre-conceived but false (and categorical) notion. Evidently man does not shine as an intuitive statistician.

CONCLUSIONS

Bruner, Goodnow and Austin (1956) suggested that all thinking, including that about people and their behaviour, tends to be categorical, yet according to Meehl's argument categorical inferences about behaviour are always incorrect in principle. People's judgements and impressions of each other are doomed to inaccuracy, unless they can be given special training in probabilistic and actuarial thinking. One might perhaps summarize by saying that Sarbin *et al.* describe how people *do* perceive others, while Meehl is describing how they *ought* to think.

The real advantage of the inference model is its fruitfulness. The intuition model does not give particularly illuminating answers to questions about person perception and has given rise to little or no research; the inference model, on the other hand, raises many interesting questions and gives a conceptual framework for a wide variety of empirical work.

## IMPLICIT PERSONALITY THEORIES

The most useful direction given to research by the inference model is the attention it draws to the general principles people have, and use to form impressions of others. Sherlock Holmes can identify someone as a typist, or a Freemason, or the King of Bohemia because he knows that typists get a double mark on both sleeves from the edge of the table, that Freemasons sometimes wear an arc and compass breastpin, and that someone who writes, in Germanic English, on paper manufactured in Bohemia, about assisting a Royal House on a delicate matter and who arrives in disguise is likely to be the King himself. Intuition approaches, by contrast, tend to ignore or deny the role of previous experience.

Most people don't have the extensive knowledge and experience of a Sherlock Holmes and couldn't recognize fifty different types of cigar ash – but everyone has a set of rules or principles for classifying people and predicting their behaviour. Also, because most people are not as able as Sherlock Holmes to describe how they reach their conclusions, these sets of rules or principles are known as '*implicit* personality theories'. Warr and Knapper (1968) call the component propositions of the theories 'inference rules'. Three different sorts of 'inference rules' can be distinguished, and these three form the subject of the next four chapters.

### Identification rules

This type of rule links visible signs to what lies behind them. The visible signs may be of the type Sherlock Holmes is so fond of describing – scuff marks on the sleeve, or mud on the boots – which lead to inferences about the person's occupation, previous movements, or future intentions. They may be something – name, skin colour, cast of features – which identifies the person as English, or Jewish, or as hailing from the upper class. Sometimes inferences are drawn from behaviour – 'girls under eighteen who smoke aren't virgins' or 'people who drive fast are impatient'. An important type of identification rule links 'non-verbal behaviour' – facial expressions, tone of voice, etc. – to the person's moods and intentions. Research on the various types of identification rule – inferences from overt behaviour, non-verbal behaviour, and stereotyped judgements based on race, class or other visible characteristics – is described in Chapters 4 and 5.

*Association rules*
Identifying someone as a doctor, or as Jewish, often leads almost immediately to further inferences about his character or likely behaviour. Some are stereotypes or examples of prejudice – Jews are mean; doctors aren't usually afraid of the sight of blood. Deciding that someone is mean or afraid of the sight of blood, commonly gives rise to further inferences still. A good Freudian will expect someone who is mean to show the two other classic traits of the 'anal personality' – orderliness and obstinacy. A behaviourist might expect fear of the sight of blood to generalize to fear of the sight of injuries, hypodermic needles, etc. Research on 'association rules' is reviewed in Chapter 6, which also discusses the problems involved in studying implicit personality theories.

*Combination rules*
Warr and Knapper (1968) point out that people usually infer from more than one cue, and that these cues may not all point the same way. Suppose someone comes into Sherlock Holmes's room, with a nitrate stain on his fingers and smelling of iodoform, but also having a copy of Chemical Abstracts visible in his pocket. Is he a doctor, or chemist or what? Warr and Knapper suggest the term 'combination rules' to describe the principles the perceiver uses – not necessarily consciously – to combine conflicting cues. Research on 'combination rules' is reviewed in Chapter 3.

INPUT SELECTION

The way a doctor looks at his patients differs from the way he looks at his wife, and from the way he looks at his bank manager; he 'selects his inputs' as Warr and Knapper put it. People with authoritarian personalities tend to be generally suspicious and fearful of others (DeSoto *et al.*, 1960) and rely more on 'external' or superficial cues (Wilkins and DeCharms, 1962). Verinis and Walker (1970) found that policemen have an eye for 'criminal detail', a finding that could probably be repeated for many other occupations. Schiffenbauer (1974) showed that emotional arousal made people see photographs of others' facial expressions as more like their own mood than they actually were, while Murray (1933), in a well-known experiment, showed that children saw faces as more evil and malicious after they had listened to a frightening ghost story. Zajonc (1960) manipulated 'cognitive tuning' – the set induced in observers before they observed a person – and found that observers who anticipated having to communicate information to others described the person in a more complex and differentiated way.

'Input selection' is a skill, as well as a stage in a model. Inferring that a man with a stethoscope is a doctor is no great achievement; noticing the stethoscope may be. A person who fails to notice significant detail simply isn't in a position to draw correct inferences. Grossman, described in Cline (1964), demonstrated this simple point, showing that subjects who couldn't remember what someone said or looked like weren't good at predicting what they would be likely to do in future, or what they thought on political issues. An eye for detail is no use however, if its owner draws the wrong inference; Giedt (1955) showed that psychiatrists commonly went wrong when diagnosing from filmed interviews, by reading too much into hesitation or restlessness and supposing they indicated the patient was chronically anxious, not temporarily nervous.

## The social skill model

Sarbin *et al.*'s inference model was devised to explain clinical judgement and psychiatric diagnosis. Can it account for judgements being made during social interactions? In fact it combines quite neatly with the social skill model of Argyle and Kendon (1967), illustrated in Figure 2.1.

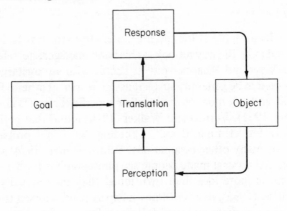

*Figure* 2.1   Argyle and Kendon's social skill model.

The social skill model is an analogy with motor skills and assumes there are four basic processes operating during interaction. The individual *perceives* the other person, decides what to do (*translation*) in order to achieve his *goal*, does it (*response*) and then examines the result (*feedback*). Suppose the person's goal is to borrow money. He sees that the other person is unwilling, because he fears he might not be repaid; experience suggests that the best response is to offer assurances, and possibly security, that the money will be repaid. He does this and observes continued reluctance and decides that the other person is now afraid of being left short of money; he points out that he only wants to borrow a small sum. He continues trying new tactics until he gets his loan, or gives up.

Expanding the 'perception' box of Argyle and Kendon's model to include an inference process (Figure 2.2) points to one significant difference between the two. The inference model stops once a judgement has been made, but the skill model takes account of the person's subsequent behaviour. In psychology experiments people commonly form opinions about other people whom they see on film and never meet, so the judgement has no consequence; in real life opinions are formed for some purpose, about people the person knows and has dealings with. Frijda (1969) reported that his subjects never spontaneously described photographs of emotional expressions in abstract terms, like those normally imposed on the subject in such experiments; they said that *someone* was doing *something* to the person in the

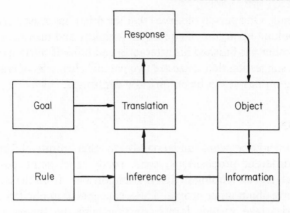

*Figure* 2.2 Expanded version of social skill model.

photographs, not simply that he was 'angry' or 'afraid'.

Forming impressions of people is not usually a 'one-off' process. The first impression shapes the first response, that has an effect on the other person, which is in turn perceived and acted on, and so on. The process is continuous and circular, so long as the encounter lasts. It is also faster than this account makes it sound. One of the features of skilled motor performance is that perception and response phases merge, so the lathe operator is looking – literally – forward to the next stage of his machining work while making the motor movements for the previous one.

*Regulation*
Argyle and Kendon make the interesting suggestion that there are two levels to perceiving other people while talking to them; at the 'higher' level judgements are made about the other's behaviour, while on the 'lower' level, the person is perceiving and responding to 'maintenance' or 'regulation' cues. In most conversations people manage not to interrupt each other or leave silences, to remain facing each other and to look at appropriate moments and so forth. Their gestures and facial movements tend to be synchronized, although the purpose of this is not known. Argyle (1969) suggests that this process of 'maintenance' or 'regulation' occurs parallel with perception of the other's moods, intentions, etc., and doesn't use the same channel, even though the 'regulation' process operates in the same way as the other

judgements. One person observes that the other has ceased speaking and is looking up at him, so he infers – rapidly and unconsciously – that the other has finished his utterance, and himself starts speaking. Argyle's suggestion that there are two parallel channels, operating in conversation has yet to be empirically confirmed.

## Summary

The argument that people understand each other 'intuitively' involves several different propositions, some partly true, some positively unhelpful, and all tending to divert attention away from the concepts people have about other people. These concepts or implicit personality theories take various forms, starting with the superficial and leading on to less obvious aspects of behaviour and personality. The starting point may be a single piece of information, or a combination of different facts. Implicit personality theories in various forms are the subject of the next four chapters, which look at what information people use, and how they use it.

# 3 PUTTING THE PIECES TOGETHER

## Processing multiple cues

> The ideal candidate would reply . . . 'Admiral Parker is
> my uncle. My father is Captain Foley, my grandfather
> Commodore Foley. My mother's father was Admiral
> Hardy. Commander Hardy is my uncle. My eldest brother
> is a lieutenant in the Royal Marines, my next brother is a
> cadet at Dartmouth and my younger brother wears a sailor
> suit' . . .
> 'And what made you think of joining the Navy?'
>
> From *The Short List* by
> C. Northcote Parkinson

The discussion in Chapter 2 of how people reach conclusions about
each other was rendered a little artificial by restricting it to the case
where inferences are drawn from only one piece of information.
Outside the unreal world of the psychology experiment, people
usually have lots of information to go on; the question is how do they
use it? A substantial body of research, carried out in several not
particularly clearly related traditions, has provided some of the
answers.

The simple case is where the various bits of information point the
same way; this raises only a few issues. Where the items of information available point in different directions, more questions need an
answer. How does the perceiver use the information he has? Does he
use it sensibly or does he waste it? Does he give the same weight to
every cue? If not, how does he decide what cues matter more? Does
the human perceiver have an edge over more mechanistic ways of
combining data, or is some sort of system better than the human
judge? The latter issue is of obvious practical relevance, as well as
theoretical interest.

**Information that all points the same way**

Northcote Parkinson's would-be naval officer made things easy for the selection board by providing eight indications of his suitability for a commission, all pointing the same way. It might be argued that the more relevant information, leading to the same conclusion, is available, the more quickly and definitely a decision ought to be reached, although the 'discounting principle' of attribution theory, described in Chapter 5, suggests that the information would be more convincing if it did not all come from the candidate. However, even in this apparently simple case, there are several theories about the way pieces of consistent information are combined.

ANDERSON'S ADJECTIVES

Before going any further, a word on one of the most popular paradigms is in order. Asch's (1946) subjects imagined a person who was 'intelligent, skilful, industrious, warm, determined, practical, cautious', wrote a personality sketch of him, and then rated him on a series of scales. Asch demonstrated that changing 'warm' to 'cold' in the list altered the whole impression created, and in doing so, stated a long tradition of research using lists of two or more trait names and rating scales. Anderson (1968) amassed 555 such adjectives and had them rated for likeableness by 100 students. He was then in a position to study various ways of predicting the overall likeability of an imaginary person, described by two or more of his adjectives, from the likeableness values of the component adjectives.

ADDING OR AVERAGING?

One of Anderson's first experiments (Anderson, 1965) compared adding and averaging models, for adjectives pointing in the same general direction. The distinction is clear; according to the adding model, the more adjectives the better, for each one will contribute something extra to the overall impression, while the averaging model in its simplest form predicts that the total number of adjectives is irrelevant, for what counts is their mean value. The crucial test of the theories is to add to an existing set of adjectives another of lesser value than the average of the set; according to the adding model the inference will be more extreme, while according to the averaging model it will be less extreme. The results of several studies of this type seem to support the averaging hypothesis, but not that positively. For example, Anderson (1965) found that combinations of four very favourable adjectives like 'reasonable, truthful, enthusiastic, original' led to a more positive inference than 'reasonable and truthful', which appears to support the adding model, but also that 'reasonable and truthful' led to a more positive inference than two very favourable adjectives and two fairly favourable adjectives, such as 'reasonable, truthful, painstaking and persuasive'. The addition of the not quite so favourable adjectives – 'painstaking' and 'persuasive' – reduced the impact of the highly favourable pair, but the addition of another highly favourable pair enhanced it, apparently contrary to the averaging theory. Anderson argues that this can be explained by postulating an initial impression, which contributes to the weighted average of the two or four adjectives. If this hypothetical initial impression is fairly neutral, then adding four highly favourable adjectives, as opposed to two, will lead to a more favourable impression. This hypothesis could be tested by measuring what subjects initially thought of a man without qualities – 'a person' – before being told he or she was 'reasonable, truthful, painstaking and original'.

## THE VALIDITY OF ANDERSON'S PARADIGM

Anderson's critics often question whether findings obtained with adjective lists would generalize to more 'lifelike' material. Anderson and Lopez (1974) showed that the averaging model applies to adverb-adjective-noun combinations, such as 'very humourous lawyer'. Rosnow (1970) compared the adding and averaging model using incomes as the cues, and status as the inference; where the various incomes all belonged to one person or one family, the additive model applies. For photographs, however, being judged for friendliness, the opposite was found (Rosnow and Arms, 1968); for photographs of women, the average of a group of three or four photographs determined the final ratings. Lampel and Anderson (1968) paired adjectives and photographs and found that words and pictures did not average out, but rather that words only added to the impression, if the picture was of an attractive person. The value of extra information evidently depends on such factors as the degree of redundancy, and the type of information being supplied.

In clinical studies – the other major tradition – the finding emerges fairly clearly that extra information is not helpful. Sines (1959) showed that predictions of a patient's Q sort[1] could be made as accurately as they ever could be from a Biographical Data Sheet; adding a Minnesota Multiphasic Personality Inventory (MMPI)[2] profile did not improve accuracy and adding a Rorschach actually reduced it. Nystedt and Magnusson (1972) similarly found that four test protocols lead to no more accurate inferences than two, while six actually produces a decline in accuracy. Too much information – especially about ambiguous tests of low validity like the Rorschach – appears to confuse the clinical expert. Goldberg (1970) lists several more studies all confirming this.

## Information that points in different directions

Unfortunately for naval officer selection boards, and other professional experts, the available information usually does not all point the same way. What is the selection board to make of a candidate from a long line of naval officers, who is keen, alert, smart and fit in every respect but one – he suffers badly from sea-sickness? And how are they to decide between the two average to mediocre candidates, one of whom is useless at arithmetic, and hence at elementary navigation, and the other of whom has a speech impediment which makes his orders unintelligible? There are as many as seven strategies for dealing with inconsistent information of this sort.

### (1)   FAVOURITE CUE OR CUES

The story of the personnel man who left selection of staff to his dog – who liked some people and growled at others – is probably apocryphal, but anyone who has had any experience in the personnel field will have come across 'experts' who 'swear by' a particular cue, and think so highly of it they largely ignore the rest of the information.

### (2)   ADDING AND (3) AVERAGING, WEIGHTED OR UNWEIGHTED

Adding and averaging amount to the same thing when the number of cues is constant. The individual items might be treated as equivalent, so that, for a naval officer candidate, physical fitness, smartness of appearance, verbal intelligence, spatial intelligence, and motivation all count equally; however, in most cases, some items carry more

---

[1]   see page 106.
[2]   A standard test of nine psychiatric syndromes.

weight than others. The weighting may be made consciously, based on the known validity of the cue or its supposed relevance, or unconsciously, reflecting the judge's experience and biases.

Several adjective-list studies have shown that the weighted average model generally applies when the adjectives are a mixture of positive and negative (Warr, 1974). Several researchers have found it necessary to note that implausible combinations lead to incredulity and 'discounting'; a person cannot be 'honest' *and* 'deceitful', and the two do not average out. Osgood, Suci and Tannenbaum (1957) refer to 'pessimistic, evaluative stickiness', meaning that unfavourable parts of a description tend to carry more weight. It is important to note that the research shows only that a weighted average model gives a fairly good fit to the ratings people make of combinations of items and doesn't prove that the raters are, consciously or unconsciously, using a weighted average strategy to produce their rating.

Discounting of one set of information usually seems to happen when what is *said* conflicts with the *way it is said*. Argyle, Alkema and Gilmour (1971) found that facial expression, tone of voice and other non-verbal cues carried far more weight in determining impressions of friendliness than did the spoken message, confirming the results of studies by Mehrabian (Mehrabian and Ferris, 1967; Mehrabian and Wiener, 1967). Bugenthal (1974) confirmed that tone of voice largely determined the impression created by a message, *unless* the speaker was seen to be 'weighing his words' – speaking with a slow, deliberate, polished delivery – in which case his tone of voice was discounted.

## (4) LINEAR REGRESSION

A weighted average of fitness, smartness, verbal intelligence, spatial intelligence and motivation might well overlook the fact that there is redundancy in the information. The two aspects of intelligence will correlate quite highly, so that assigning an equal weight to each would give undue weight to intelligence overall. Motivation, on the other hand, might well be unrelated to the other factors, except possibly smartness, so that it contributes fresh information. The Second World War selection research provides real examples of this – adding a test of general intelligence to a battery of tests for pilots of bomber planes increased the overall validity of selection by a mere 0.002 (Cronbach, 1960).

A linear regression analysis takes account of redundancy in correlation between the cues, and ensures that what is effectively the same information is not counted twice. It may be recalled that Meehl (1961), criticizing Sarbin *et al.*'s account of inferences about people, argued that a regression approach was more suitable, because it could handle multiple cues more efficiently. Evidence summarized in the previous chapter indicated that naïve observers were poor at thinking in terms of less than perfect correlations, or one to one correspondences. However, an impressive body of research, mostly on clinical judgements, generally shows that linear regression seems to predict the results of clinicians' deliberations most accurately, which does not of course prove that that is how the clinicians drew their conclusions.

Recently Dawes and Corrigan (1974) have cast doubt on the need to calculate regressions, and argue that giving equal weight to each cue – in effect using a sum or average – generally gives just as good a result; tests on artifical data, and one or two earlier studies, confirm their argument.

(5)  CONFIGURAL JUDGEMENTS, INCLUDING (6) MULTIPLE CUT-OFF AND (7) SINGLE DISQUALIFYING CUE

Given the necessary data, the calculation of a linear regression is a simple, mechanical process, taking only a few seconds with a modern calculator. If the input data are collected 'mechanically', from personality tests, or biographical material, the 'expert' becomes redundant and his place can be taken by a semi-skilled clerk or even a computer console. The clinical expert defends his position by arguing that a linear regression ignores the subtleties of his thought processes and imposes a crude oversimplified model on the data. The argument goes back to Asch (1946), a Gestalt psychologist, who explained his 'warm/cold' effect, by arguing that changing 'warm' to 'cold' produced a qualitive meaning change in the other adjectives; intelligence in a warm person meant something different from intelligence in a cold person. Thorndike even earlier (1918) made the same point, and wondered if the value of technical skill might not vary as a square function of intelligence – virtually useless in a stupid person, but immensely valuable in a genius. A linear regression could take no account of this. Similarly degrees of ill health are quite an important consideration to a personnel manager, whereas degrees of good health, above that needed for the work, are relatively unimportant.

The linear regression model, like the averaging model, allows a candidate to compensate for his weak points, by being particularly strong on others. However, models (6) and (7), which are essentially configural – where the conclusion depends on the overall pattern of configuration of the elements – do not allow such compensation. Model (7), the single disqualifying cue, often influences employment decisions. A criminal record is an absolute bar to many occupations; foreign origin is likely to be for a would-be naval officer. This principle is sometimes extended to give model (6), the multiple cut-off system, in which minimal qualifications are set on each cue; Cronbach (1960) cites the example of an American sonar operator course in the Second World War that found it necessary to specify a minimum standard of pitch discrimination, without which the candidate could not be accepted regardless of his other qualities.

CLINICAL VERSUS STATISTICAL PREDICTION

The question of configural cues is an important issue in the dispute between statistical or actuarial prediction, and clinical judgement. Much of the research in this dispute uses a standard paradigm, distinguishing between psychosis and neurosis on the basis of over 1,200 MMPI profiles collected from all over the USA by Meehl (1959).

Meehl (1954) published a review of research on psychiatric diagnosis, choice of treatment, parole violations, selection for clinical work, and other predictive tasks, showing that statistical or actuarial methods were always as good as, and usually better than, clinical methods. The actuarial method will be familiar to anyone who is insured to drive a car; one's premium (or in extreme cases eligibility for insurance) is calculated from a standard table that takes account of factors the insurer knows from experience to be relevant – age, occupation, type of car, place of residence, and previous accident and conviction record. This method was applied to assessing suitability for parole for imprisoned offenders in Massachusetts in the 1920s; Hart (1923) found that 'use of drugs' or 'father served jail sentence' were bad signs, while 'guilty of assault and battery' or 'accidental offender' were relatively good signs. Many similar analyses have been reported since, including the research of Mannheim and Wilkins (1955) on the prediction of further juvenile delinquency in Britain. The constructor of such a table works on a purely empirical basis; if factor A which seems very relevant does not predict further offending, while factor B which seems quite irrelevant does, factor B is included, not factor A. Once the 'actuarial tables' have been drawn up and appropriate weights assigned to relevant cues, the predictions can be made the way motor insurance premiums are calculated, by a semi-skilled clerk reading off a standard table.

The essence of the clinical approach is by contrast, to quote Gough (1962), that 'the combining is done intuitively . . . hypotheses and constructs are generated during the course of the analysis . . . and the process is mediated by an individual's judgement and reflection'. The clinical judgements discussed by Meehl (1954) and others since are made by experts – clinical psychologists, psychiatrists and social workers – but most day-to-day judgements are made in the same way. The judge reaches a conclusion about someone from some or all of the available information but is not necessarily able to say what cues he uses or how much weight he attaches to each. The clinical method has great appeal, both to its practitioners and to many sections of the public. An effort is seen to be made to study the individual as an individual, an effort which could surely discover facts about him – the circumstances in which the subject's father served jail sentences perhaps – which would throw new light on his suitability for parole; an actuarial table by contrast seems crude, inhuman and bureaucratic.

However, Meehl was unable to find any evidence that the clinical method led to more accurate assessment, and, since his review, little has emerged to challenge his conclusions that the statistical method – the 'cookbook' as Meehl puts it – is better. Lindzey (1965) reported a study showing that clinical prediction of male homosexuality from Thematic Apperception Test (TAT)[1] protocols was slightly better than a formula based on twenty TAT signs; however the difference was nowhere near statistically significant. Otherwise the study of Young (1972) is typical; MMPI profiles where a set of decision rules – the 'Goldberg rules' (Goldberg, 1965) – could not tell diagnosed neurotics from diagnosed psychotics were equally baffling to clinicians. The clinician could not take over where the rules left off nor, as has been shown in other studies, was the clinician's confidence related to his accuracy.

Sawyer (1966) makes the point that the statistical method – the 'cookbook' – does not have to be as simple as a weighted average or linear regression. The formula can be as complicated as the data

---

[1]   A projective test of personality.

demand, especially now that computers and sophisticated calculators are generally available. Kleinmuntz (1963) has constructed programs for coding MMPI profiles, based on the way clinical experts describe their own thought processes. There are a number of other non-linear rules for coding MMPI profiles, some elaborate, like the 'Meehl-Dahlstrom rules', others very simple like the 'High-Point-Rule', which says 'if the highest score is on Hysteria, Depression, Hypochondria, or Psychasthenia, the patient is neurotic; if not, he is psychotic'.

## MAN VERSUS MODEL OF MAN

Some studies (Goldberg, 1970; Dawes and Corrigan, 1974) infer the expert's rules by analysing his use of the cues, rather than by asking him directly. Deriving a set of rules describing, or at least reproducing, the way the expert works, and then comparing the rules' predictions with his further judgements yields a result that, at first, is very surprising. The rule-derived predictions are more consistently accurate than the expert they are derived from; a statistical 'model of man' is better than the man himself. The superiority of a model of a judge over the judge himself has been demonstrated for predictions of neurosis/psychosis from the MMPI (Goldberg, 1970) and for predictions of grade-point-average from nine varyingly relevant cues (Wiggins and Kohen, 1971). Dawes and Corrigan (1974) call this 'bootstrapping' – the apparently impossible feat of lifting oneself up by one's own bootstraps. The obvious explanation of how 'bootstrapping' works, once one knows that it does, is that the formula is absolutely consistent, and never has off-days, moods, or lapses of attention. Dawes and Corrigan argue, however, that any system of weighting the cues gives as good results as a set of weights derived from the expert judge's judgements. Giving equal weight to each one and not bothering to calculate a regression equation gave even better results. This seems to imply that the expert's weighting of the cues is inaccurate, and that all he is contributing to the task of prediction is an intelligent choice of cues to use.

## ARE CONFIGURAL JUDGEMENTS NECESSARY?

While the actuarial formula can be as complicated as is necessary, the bulk of research shows that usually it need not be any more elaborate than a linear regression. Meehl (1959) did find that neurotic and psychotic MMPI profiles could be best distinguished by the 'highly configural' Meehl-Dahlstrom rules, which were superior to simple linear models. For example, the 'mania' scale did not contribute much to linear predictions of psychosis, because some psychotics had high scores, and others very low, whereas, according to one of the Meehl-Dahlstrom rules, high mania, coupled with very low scores on the other scales, especially hypochondria, depression and hysteria, was a near infallible indicator of psychosis. However, Meehl's result seems exceptional and several studies since, using the MMPI (Goldberg, 1965), or predicting parole violations (Babst, Gottfredson and Ballard, 1968; Pritchard, 1977), have found that linear methods give the best predictions.

## DO PEOPLE MAKE CONFIGURAL JUDGEMENTS?

The work of Goldberg, Pritchard and Gottfredson suggested that one does not usually need elaborate configural strategies to get the right answer; other research at the Oregon Research Institute makes it doubtful whether expert judges actually make configural judgements very often. These studies employ analysis of variance to detect configural use of cues; if an expert predicting parole violation from type of offence and age thinks that a crime of violence is a bad sign for a young offender, but not for an older person, this would show up as an interaction in an analysis of variance of his predictions. Rorer *et al.*'s (1967) judges – nurses, doctors, psychologists and social workers – assessed psychiatric inpatients' suitability for a weekend pass from six systematically varied cues. Some interactions were found, indicating configural judgement, but overall only 2 percent of the variance was accounted for by interactions. Judges varied a lot in their strategies; quite a few restricted themselves to a simple linear combination of three out of six cues, while others used up to twenty-two interactions, including interactions of up to five items. There was no criterion data – whether the patients really were suitable for leave – in Rorer *et al.*'s study; Wiggins and Hoffman (1968) used Meehl's MMPI profiles, where data of actual neurosis/psychosis were available. Sixteen of the twenty-nine judges did use cues configurally, but were not more – nor less – accurate as a consequence. Hoffman, Slovic and Rorer (1968) studied the use of five cues on X-ray photographs indicating an ulcer and found, like Rorer *et al.*, little evidence of configural judgements being extensively used. The only type of expert studied so far who used cues configurally on any scale is the stockbroker, predicting growth potential of his stocks from eleven cues (Slovic, 1969).

## CONCLUSIONS

So far it appears that the expert is no better than a formula, that he does not make much use of configural cues and that he does not have much cause to, because valid cues to the things he is predicting are rarely configural. None of this means that the expert is redundant, rather than he would be more usefully employed than in making predictions from ready-made data like the MMPI, where a formula is easily constructed. As Meehl (1959) pointed out, the clinical psychologist's task is often much less structured than saying 'neurotic/psychotic'; often 'the very content of the prediction has to be produced by the predictor'. Further, the clinician adds to the MMPI data observations on the patient's behaviour while completing the test. The conclusion remains however that, while the clinical expert may be good at collecting the data, he is probably wasting his time and lowering his accuracy, if he attempts to combine more than a few items of information, without the aid of some formula or other statistical crutch. If the expert's decision-making is so limited, it is likely that the layman, even if he fares no worse, is unlikely to fare better.

# PART II
# SOURCES OF INFORMATION
# IN PERCEIVING OTHER
# PEOPLE

Chapters 2 and 3 came to the conclusion that opinions about other people have as their starting points premises, from which further conclusions are inferred. These starting points can be facial expressions, skin colour or surname, or can be meaningful actions, such as an attack on another, or an act of generosity, or can be an already formed opinion, as in the case of the opinion 'X is intelligent' leading to the opinion 'therefore he has emotional problems'.

The diverse and uneven body of research and speculations dealing with what information people use is discussed in the next three chapters. Work on superficial characteristics is discussed in Chapter 4, work on meaningful sequences of behaviour is discussed in Chapter 5, while work on the inference of one personality trait from another is described in Chapter 6. The research is diverse and uneven because it uses a variety of different experimental models, or because some of it was conducted primarily to answer questions in other fields of psychology. Virtually all the research on how people interpret each others' action has been conducted within the framework of 'attribution theory'.

# PART II
## SOURCES OF INFORMATION
## IN PERCEIVING OTHER
## PEOPLE

# 4 INFORMATION RECEIVED

## Inferences from superficial characteristics

> Gradually like a herd of big game scenting man, the members of the Committee began turning heads in my direction. As each gaze reached my face it became keen and searching, and soon they were all engaged in that activity which Welshmen love and in which, more than most things, they like to think they excel; summing the fellow up.
>
> From *That Uncertain Feeling* by
> Kingsley Amis

This chapter will consider what information people actually use, as well as what information they might use, when reaching conclusions about each other. The first stage of the person perception process is the inference from visible or specific details to what lies behind them – the 'identification rule' part of the 'implicit personality theory'. The greater part of the research on 'identification rules' falls into two major categories – the study of stereotypes, and the analysis of 'non-verbal communication'.

## Stereotypes

Amis's fictional interview board are deluding themselves about their powers of observation; the reliable information to be gained from looking at someone is limited and mostly superficial – nothing, that in an interview, would not already be on the application form. Stereotyped judgements of this sort can be based on age, occupation and sex, as well as on appearance.

MEASURING STEREOTYPES

Much of the research has used the method pioneered by Katz and Braly (1933) to measure racial stereotypes. Katz and Braly found that 84 percent of Princeton students thought Negroes superstitious and 75 percent thought them lazy. The students expressed equally clear opinions about many other races, including ones they had never met, and were unlikely to, such as Turks. Katz and Braly's results are not so much proof of the bigotry of American students, as of their willingness to perform any task labelled 'psychology experiment'. As Brigham (1971) points out, when a subject in a Katz and Braly type study is given a sheet of paper headed 'The American Negro' and asked to check which of eighty-four adjectives apply, his only sensible – non-stereotyping – response is to refuse to do the experiment. Eysenck and Crown (1948) found that 19 percent of their subjects did just that, and many more expressed doubts about the task.

This is not to say that stereotypes do not exist, but to argue that a slightly subtler way of measuring them is needed. One favourite method is to present subjects with a photograph, and to ask them to describe the person portrayed in it, and then to vary that person's characteristics. For example, Hess (1965) had the same photograph of an attractive girl rated by students in two guises, one with dilated pupils and one with contracted pupils; he found the dilated pupils caused the girl to be seen as more attractive and more sexually motivated. Secord, Bevan and Katz (1956) had high-school pupils rate ten pictures of Negroes, ranging from 100 percent Negro ancestry through to largely white ancestry and, in Atlanta, Georgia, proved the truth of the old racist principle that any admixture, however small, of Negro ancestry makes a person a Negro, not a white. All ten pictures were rated as equally 'superstitious, lazy, emotional and immoral'. It is also possible to prove that someone's appearance has an immediate impact by field studies using 'unobtrusive measures'. A Negro asking a white American for change is less likely to get it (Raymond and Unger, 1972), just as a 'lost letter' addressed to an obviously Negro person is less likely to be posted on (Benson, Karabenick and Lerner, 1976) by people who 'find' it in a telephone box.

INFORMATION ON WHICH STEREOTYPES MAY BE BASED

Because the variation-on-a-photographic-theme experiment is easy to do, it has been done for a great variety of cues; it has been shown that hair colour (Lawson, 1971), beardedness (Kenny and Fletcher, 1973), dress (Gibbins, 1969; Coursey, 1973), physical attractiveness (Miller, 1970), physique (Strongman and Hart, 1968), make-up (McKeachie, 1952), wearing of glasses (Thornton, 1944) all affect the impression created. It is equally easy to create variations in tape-recorded voices, and studies on regional accents have been reported by Tucker and Lambert (1969), among others. Earlier research, reviewed by Kramer (1963), had shown that attempts to rate personality or identify a person's occupation from his or her voice were often systematically wrong, indicating the existence of stereotyped but false ideas about what a clergyman, or an extrovert should sound like. Even more minimal information than a photograph or a voice can suffice to evoke a stereotype. American students agree that Michael and James are nice, masculine, bright sounding names, whereas Percival is none of these, just as Wendy is a nice, feminine, bright name, while Alfreda and Isidore are not (Buchanan and Bruning, 1971).

Lately, sex-role stereotypes have become a main focus of interest and it has been shown that many inferences are drawn from a knowledge of a person's sex; Cohen and Bunker (1975) found that women were cast as likely candidates for the post of 'editorial assistant' while men were seen as good 'personnel technicians'. Rosen and Jerdee (1974) found women discriminated against for management positions. These studies used the 'application form' method, similar to the variations-of-a-photograph technique; subjects rate applications in which every relevant detail remains constant and only the applicant's sex is varied. Content analysis of books and films is often used; Hillman (1974) showed that children's books of the 1930s showed men as physically aggressive, and competent, while women were affiliative, dependent and often sad. Unlike ethnic stereotypes, sex-role stereotypes had not changed in a 1970 sample of children's books.

CRITICISMS OF STEREOTYPES

Lippman (1922) introduced the term: 'we pick out what our culture has already defined for us, and we tend to perceive that which we have picked out in the form stereotyped for us by our culture.' He pointed out some of the ways in which stereotypes can be misleading, and since his analysis most psychologists who have written about stereotypes have given the impression of disapproving of them – the very word has a pejorative ring. Criticisms of stereotypes take several forms, as follows.

### Stereotypes as logical fallacies

It is argued that people who use stereotypes often fall into logical fallacies; they equate an accurate generalization like 'American Negroes are poorer on the whole' with 'All American Negroes are poor' (the 'exceptionless generalization') or even with the absurd proposition 'Every American Negro is poorer than every American white' (the 'no-overlap' principle). In fact Mann (1967) found that only one in six white South Africans were prepared to say things about 'All Africans' as opposed to 80/60/40 percent of Africans. Another criticism of stereotypes is less sensible; it is said that stereotyped ideas are 'received' or taken on trust, and not based on experience. In fact the same is true of most of human knowledge.

### Stereotypes as incorrect

Katz and Braly started another line of thought about why stereotyped thinking is undesirable; they complained that 'a stereotype . . . conforms very little to the facts it tends to represent.' In their rush to deny any possibility whatever that American Negroes could be superstitious, dirty, or lazy, social scientists overlook the fact that there is very little systematic evidence of national and racial differences, so that while it is unlikely that groups have all or any of the characteristics attributed to them, it would be premature to dismiss the possibility out of hand. The 'grain of truth' hypothesis has been shown to be correct, occasionally at least; in a survey of stereotyping by different African tribal groups of each other, Campbell (1967) noted that stereotypes of the Luo always brought in the fact that they, unlike their neighbours, do not practise circumcision.

Stereotypes based on things the person has some control over – clothes, beard, hair – have a much better chance of being true. Jahoda (1963) showed that the stereotyped idea that people who wear glasses are more intelligent was partially true; perhaps more intelligent people read more and so discover, or even create, a need for glasses.

### Stereotypes as rigid

Another criticism Katz and Braly made of stereotypes was that they were 'fixed', rigid, unchanged and perhaps unchangeable by contrary evidence. Racial stereotypes, according to one popular line of thought, are bound to be like that, because they arise from the individual's need to project his own repressed aggression and forbidden sexual impulses onto minority groups (see for example Adorno *et al.*, 1950). However, racial stereotypes do change gradually. Americans' ideas about Germans and Japanese changed for the worse between 1933 and 1950 (Gilbert, 1951) while their willingness to form stereotypes at all had declined by 1970 (Sisley, 1970). Stereotypes based on appearance seem far from rigid, according to Argyle and McHenry (1971); five minutes interview time was enough to eliminate the 'glasses and intelligence' stereotype completely, even though it has a 'grain of truth'.

It is conceivable that sex-role stereotypes or ethnic stereotypes are clung to for psycho-dynamic or even for economic reasons – but could this explain why a man wearing clerical garb is rated differently (Coursey, 1973), or why football coaches have stereotyped ideas about the personalities typical of backs and forwards (Williams and Yousef, 1972)? Discounting for the moment the 'grain of truth' hypothesis, there remains Brigham's suggestion, which follows on the line of argument of earlier chapters. In order to deal with a world which is too complex for direct acquisition man constructs a 'picture inside his head' of the world beyond his reach. It will be recalled that Chapman and Chapman (1967) found both experts and laymen very ready to impose false categorical notions on what they saw, and very reluctant to abandon them in the face of contrary evidence. Recall also Bruner's argument that thinking generally uses categorical terms – all Negroes/Canadians/women are . . . – and Meehl's points that such a line of thought is inevitably misleading.

## Non-verbal communication

Once a person ceases to be a static display, and starts behaving, he becomes a more useful source of information. An earlier generation of psychologists paid relatively little attention to 'expressive behaviour' as they called it, but since 1965 a steadily increasing flow of experiments, reviews and critiques has appeared in the literature. Most of this research has concentrated on discovering what non-verbal behaviour actually means, as opposed to what people think it means.

DETERMINING THE INFERENCES DRAWN FROM NON-VERBAL
BEHAVIOUR

There are subtle and crude ways of finding how people interpret each
other's non-verbal behaviour. This observation – which holds for
most sorts of implicit personality theory – applies particularly to
non-verbal behaviour, where subtlety is especially required, and is
conspicuous by its absence for the most part. A common failing of
much of the early research on non-verbal communication (NVC),
particularly that on facial expression, was to assume that each expression meant something, and that that something was necessarily an
emotional state; a good judge of facial expression was someone who
could apply the right label to each expression. Many wholly artificial
experiments were performed within this tradition, in which subjects
looked at still photographs – mostly monochrome – of grotesque
posed expressions and chose from a list of words like 'angry', 'happy',
'sad'. Apart from its many obvious faults, this type of research overlooks the fact that the face conveys more information than the emotional state of its owner.

Other research has employed methods similar to those used to
study stereotypes – a standard presentation is varied in one or more
ways and the effect of the variations on free descriptions and ratings
analysed; in a typical study Argyle, Lefebvre and Cook (1974) studied
the ratings made of people who varied the amount they looked at
another person. This technique yields useful data, so long as the
experimenter does not expose the same subject to so many variations
on a particular theme as to lose his interest, or to allow him to guess the
hypothesis.

Some research favours less direct methods, preferring to study the
non-verbal response to non-verbal behaviour; Kendon (1970) has
established that non-verbal behaviour of two people talking is often
synchronized, in a way that could communicate something to them.
He has also studied the way in which non-verbal cues, especially
gestures and shifts of posture, relate to the structure of what is being
said – which could also communicate something to the listener.
Inasmuch as people make use of non-verbal behaviour of this sort, it
can be regarded as an example of an implicit personality theory – more
implicit, and less open to introspection and verbal report, than most
perhaps.

THE MESSAGES CONVEYED BY NON-VERBAL BEHAVIOUR

Argyle *et al.* (1970) found that the non-verbal elements of a message about the subject's attitude to the judge carried far more weight than the content of the message. On the other hand, two studies have found that visual information is not used much (Giedt, 1955) or is positively unhelpful (Maier and Thurber, 1968), when judges were rating personality characteristics of the subjects. Argyle *et al.* (1970) suggest that interpersonal attitudes are conveyed non-verbally and there is a taboo on expressing them verbally.

Ekman and Friesen (1969) distinguish other functions of NVC besides conveying attitudes or emotions.

*Emblems*
Some non-verbal cues are 'emblems' – signals that are given deliberately and which have a specific meaning that can be translated directly into words. Typical 'emblems' are shaking the fist to indicate anger or nodding the head to show assent.

*Illustrators*
Some non-verbal cues are 'illustrators' – gestures and movements that the speaker makes to separate the successive parts of his discourse and which could be thought of almost as a system of visual punctuation. They also expand and clarify the content, indicating spatial relationships, drawing the object mentioned, pointing to the object, or to the speaker's relationship to it, and so on. Kendon (1972) examined the use of such 'illustrators' and finds that the speaker's movements do correspond to the structure of what he says, with a hierarchy of movements in different parts of the body paralleling a hierarchical structure of what he says; shifts in the trunk or legs only occur at the ends of paragraphs, while movements of the hands and forearm tend to occur at every phrase. Kendon also finds that movements are associated with the speech content, as well as its structure; pronouns referring to the speaker are often accompanied by a gesture moving towards the speaker, while other pronouns are accompanied by gestures moving away from the speaker. These movements do not communicate anything in themselves, but help the listener attend to and understand what is being said.

*Regulators*

Somewhat similar movements and gestures are made by the listener, indicating how he is reacting to the speaker. These 'regulators' have been studied by Scheflen (1965) and others in a somewhat unsystematic way. Head nods, raising the eyebrows, slight postural shifts can indicate to the speaker that the listener is interested or not, wants him to go faster, or repeat something, or change the subject, or stop. Verbal conditioning studies (Krasner, 1958) have shown that head nods, as well as their verbal equivalents, can make the speaker say more while their absence can make him say less.

*Adaptors*

Finally, Ekman and Friesen suggest that some gestures occur because they were learned as useful, and have remained part of the subject's behaviour, although they no longer serve any purpose. Such 'adaptors' are likely to be idiosyncratic, so their significance can only be learned by acquaintance with the person. A study by Krout (1954) produced some relevant evidence. His subjects were put under stress and any gestures they produced were recorded. Krout found that a great variety of gestures were produced, but some occurred quite consistently and some of these were related to the subject's report of his reaction to the situation. Some of these gestures were probably 'adaptors' and were originally learned as responses to anxiety.

*Kinemes*

Birdwhistell (1968) also imposed some order on the confused mass of information provided by NVC, with the concept of the 'kineme'. This corresponds to the 'phoneme' in language – a class of sounds that are not physically but functionally identical. Just as the syllable 'cat' means the same whether spoken harshly, slowly or with a Scots accent, so a single head nod by a listener always means, according to Birdwhistell, that the person is willing to continue listening, whereas a triple head nod always indicates impatience. Birdwhistell's analysis, which is not explained very clearly anywhere, leads him to conclude that thirty-three 'kinemes' can be made with the face and head by North American speakers.

COMMUNICATION AND EXPRESSION BY NON-VERBAL
BEHAVIOUR

What a look or a gesture means or *expresses* may not correspond with
what people take it to mean, or *communicate*. The distance two people
place themselves apart for a meeting has great significance according
to the anthropological researches of Hall (1966), but laboratory
research by Porter, Argyle and Salter (1970) found that contrived
variations in distance communicated nothing to observers. Cook and
Smith (1975) found that deliberate variation in the amount of time a
confederate looked a subject in the eye exerted a relatively slight
influence on how the confederate was rated and described. Furthermore, one of the inferences drawn from not looking was that the
confederate was anxious, even though a study by Hobson *et al*. (1973)
failed to prove that people made anxious react by looking others in the
eye less.

The discrepancy between expression and communication arises
partly because people are not good at expressing their emotions, and
because others are not good at perceiving them; however, some of its
roots go deeper. Some non-verbal changes occur too fast to be perceived readily. Haggard and Isaacs (1966) identified 'micro-
momentary' changes in facial expressions, by a frame-by-frame
analysis of cine-film, and related them to imperfectly repressed hostil-
ity towards the interviewer; events lasting only 1/24 second are difficult to perceive. Other non-verbal changes involve parts of the body
that custom, clothes, or furniture prevent the observer focusing on
very readily. Ekman (1972) found that nurses trying to conceal their
true feelings about a gruesome film gave themselves away by a hand-
shrugging movement, which an observer at normal conversational
distance, following the usual custom of looking people in the eye while
listening to them, might have difficulty picking up. The same probably goes for the 'palm presentation' sign, described by Scheflen
(1965) as a highly reliable indicator, in middle-class white American
women, of a willingness to court or at least flirt.

*Ekman's theory of non-verbal behaviour*
Ekman and Friesen (1969) present an interesting theory about NVC
that helps to explain why it will often be a poor cue to someone's real
feelings (Figure 4.1). Their problem was to reconcile, on the one
hand, Darwin's theories and their own data suggesting that facial

expressions are understood across different cultures because they are innate, and on the other hand, the fact pointed to by their critics, that Europeans cannot understand the Chinese, because they are inscrutable or inexpressive, and that in some societies gestures, if not facial expressions, have the opposite meaning in the West. Ekman and Friesen made the suggestion, not very profound in itself, that both instinct and culture determine facial expression, then went on to argue that *instinct* controls the link between an emotion and its facial expression, so that happiness always produces the same expression, while *culture* determines what events cause what emotions, and what effort the person makes to control his facial and other expressions. Anthropological evidence shows that the Chinese are not 'naturally' inscrutable, but are brought up not to let their emotions show, as to a lesser extent are the British and Americans (at least they gesticulate less than the French, according to the elegant work of Sainsbury and Wood, 1977). However, the control is voluntary and is not complete; the mask can slip in a number of ways. It can slip very briefly, and be instantly replaced, or so Ekman and Friesen interpret the 'micro-momentary' expressions observed by Haggard and Isaacs (1966); it can slip from those parts of the body least under voluntary control, through nervous gestures of the hands or through a trembling of the stiff upper lip, and of course it can slip when the person thinks no one is watching. Ekman (1972) showed some specially selected horrific films to American and Japanese students, who saw them in company,

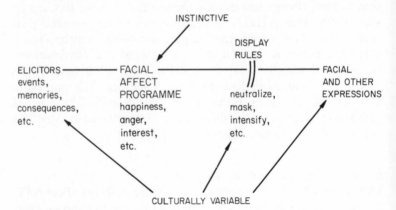

*Figure* 4.1  Ekman's model of the contributions of culture and instinct to the expression of emotion.

or on their own. Being in company made no difference to the Americans, who were equally visibly shaken in either condition, but it did make a difference for the Japanese, whose impassivity in company broke down somewhat when they were on their own to allow some limited facial expression of their horror. Control of non-verbal expression is a skill which some people have developed further than others, an an ingenious experiment by Exline *et al.* (1970) showed. College students were induced to cheat during a supposed concept formation test, and were then confronted by the experimenter who told them bluntly that their results were too good to be true. Many were unable to meet the experimenter's eye when thus confronted, but some were – the 'Machiavellian' subjects, who scored high on a 'Machiavellianism' scale, designed to identify people good at manipulating others to their own advantage.

## A CLOSER LOOK AT IMPLICIT PERSONALITY THEORIES OF GAZE DIRECTION

The research on what conclusions people draw from the readiness of others to look them in the eye yields some interesting results. In the first place not everyone seems to notice another's line of gaze; less than half did in the study by Cook and Smith (1975). Le Compte and Rosenfeld (1971) found people failed to report a slight variation in another's gaze pattern, but that it did affect how they rated the person. Apart from the obvious inference, that someone who is looking at someone else has either struck up a conversation with them, or would like to, people tend to interpret being looked at as a sign of liking. However, Argyle *et al.* (1974) found some evidence that a point of diminishing returns is reached; a continuous gaze is not quite so well-received as one that occasionally wavers. A steady gaze is also interpreted as a sign of honesty (Exline *et al.*, 1970), sincerity (Exline, 1971), and persuasiveness (Cobin and McIntyre, 1961). All these findings apply only when the person doing the looking is talking to the person forming the impressions. Looking at someone who, so to speak, has not been introduced, has quite different effects. From a man to a girl – or vice versa – it usually comes over as sexual interest. From a man to man, or from a man to a monkey, it comes over as a hostile intrusion. Ellsworth, Carlsmith and Henson (1972) found that a staring pedestrian made motorists drive off faster when the traffic lights changed; Exline's rhesus monkey attacked a staring experimenter (Exline and Yellin, 1969). There are places where looking at someone could get a person labelled a witch, especially if he or she had a squint, deep set eyes, or ones of an unusual colour; in parts of Africa the local people, the Mende, think that people who do not look at others are really ghosts (Argyle and Cook, 1976).

CONCLUSIONS

With the exception of research on facial expressions, the study of non-verbal behaviour is a recent development within the field of person perception. The best research of non-verbal behaviour has come near to doing justice to the subtlety of its subject matter, avoiding imposing the experimenter's categories on the subject's perception, and avoiding 'crystallizing' his perceptions by asking him for opinions he does not have. The emphasis on non-verbal behaviour in recent research has also avoided the artificiality of studying 'one-off ' opinions that often have no consequences for the perceiver, and which certainly do not affect his subsequent interaction with the person he is perceiving.

# 5 THE REASON WHY
## Inferences from behaviour

'She appears to be a perfectly charming little girl, well-mannered, basically unselfish. It seems that she can adapt well among children her age and make a good impression . . . she plays well with everyone, but like anyone else a bad day can occur. Her cruelty . . . need not be taken seriously.'

'I think the child would be quite bratty and would be a problem to teachers . . . she would probably try to pick a fight with other children her own age . . . she would be a brat at home . . . all in all, she would be a real problem.'

Teacher's descriptions of naughty children,
From Karen Dion (1972)

The focus of interest of those researching in person perception has shifted over the last twelve years or so, from a concern with questions like 'are his impressions correct' or 'are they systematically organized' to investigations of what people think about the reasons for their own and other people's behaviour. Do things happen through force of circumstance, or do people do things because they mean to, because they are that sort of person? Under what circumstances is someone held responsible for the things he does, and for things that happen? What ideas do people have about the reasons for success and failure? Do people make up minds about their own reasons and motives in the same way that they assess others? If not, what are the differences? 'Attribution theory' seeks to answer questions like these.

'Attribution' is unhelpfully defined by Webster's *New International Dictionary* as 'the act of attributing'; the definition of an 'attribute' is more useful: 'a quality considered as belonging to, or inherent in, a person or thing.' The choice of 'attribution' to describe the way observations of behaviour lead to judgements about personality seems to represent the same discontent with the term 'perception' as was expressed in Chapter 1. One *perceives* a hammer falling onto a foot, one takes into account the circumstances and past events, and one *attributes* the trait of clumsiness. Attribution theory focuses more particularly on the circumstances and the past events than on the present behaviour, and argues that these are more important in judging someone's behaviour than what is actually perceived, or what actually happens.

## The Theory stated

### THE ATTRIBUTION OF TRAITS TO EXPLAIN BEHAVIOUR

When someone sees a child kick a dog, he can either say the child did it because he does not like dogs or he can say something tending to excuse the action, such as 'he had to do it to protect himself' or 'he was tricked into doing it' or 'he did not mean to do it'. Attribution theory calls the former – dislike of dogs – a 'dispositional attribution', while the latter reasons are lumped together as 'situational attributions'. Many experiments have been carried out to determine how and under what circumstances a particular inference is made. The two comments quoted at the beginning of the chapter were both made by schoolteachers, and both were describing a child hitting another child in the school playground. The first teacher thinks the child a 'brat', while the second thinks her child was having a 'bad day'; the only difference between the two children was that one – the one attributed the unpleasant disposition – was physically unattractive, while the other – not seen as inherently wicked – was good-looking.

Other factors besides appearance affect the sort of inferences people draw from behaviour. Thibaut and Riecken (1955) found that high status people were regarded as making a choice when asked to do something – a dispositional inference – whereas low status people were regarded as having been persuaded – a situational inference. Jones, Davis and Gergen (1961) showed that 'out-of-role' behaviour leads to dispositional inferences; when a candidate for the post of sub-marine explorer, or astronaut, behaved in a way inconsistent with 'the ideal personality type for the job' (as described by the experimenter), observers were more likely to think that that was the real him. If he conformed to the job description, he could just be putting on a front, trying to ingratiate himself – a 'situational inference'. Another early study by De Charms, Carpenter and Kuperman (1965) showed that doing something for a popular person was more likely to be seen as a deliberate, voluntary act, than doing it for an unliked unpopular person. The effect was greater when the popular or unpopular 'other' was a small group – a 'work-crew' or 'fellow interns' – but less if the other was a large organization, such as a trade union or the American Medical Association.

Several attempts have been made to construct a conceptual framework to explain how, or even predict when, people will see acts as evidence of an underlying disposition. Heider (1958) made the first contribution. He argued that people perceive an action as resulting from a combination of factors within the person and within the environment. Factors within the person could be sub-divided into ability and effort factors – 'can' and 'tries'. Heider appears to have arrived at his conclusions from a consideration of naïve descriptions of behaviour, although he is not very explicit about this; it is in any case hard to dispute his analysis, for saying that an action results from personal and environmental forces excludes nothing and amounts to little more than saying that the action occurs. What besides personal initiative and natural causes could account for someone's behaviour?

JONES AND DAVIS'S THEORY OF CORRESPONDENT INFERENCES

Jones and Davis (1965) start with Heider's distinctions between personal and environmental forces and between ability and effort. They go on to develop the model shown in Figure 5.1; it contains two stages – the inferences from an action to an intention and from an intention to a disposition. To infer that someone meant to do something because he's like that, is to make a 'correspondent inference' – the disposition corresponds to the intention and the intention corresponds to the action. Factors which tend to make people produce correspondent inferences include – using Jones and Davis's terms – 'hedonic relevance', low 'social desirability', and 'non-common effects'. Factors which tend to make people arrive at non-correspondent inferences – 'he didn't mean to do it' or 'he isn't really like that' – include 'perceived inability', high 'social desirability', 'personalism', and 'discounting effects'. This confusion of technical terms needs to be clarified with some examples.

*Social desirability*

If someone does something that has bad consequences or is frowned

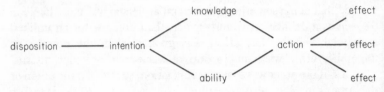

*Figure* 5.1  Jones and Davis's theory of correspondent inferences.

upon, onlookers are more likely to think he meant to do it, than if he does something conventional and acceptable. Accepting a drink from one's host reveals nothing, whereas throwing it in his face does.

### Hedonic relevance

This refers to the effect the person's behaviour has on the perceiver. If one is affected pleasantly or unpleasantly by someone's behaviour, one is more likely to see the behaviour as intentional and typical. In the drink throwing example, the host, as target of the action, is more likely to make a correspondent inference than the onlookers.

### Personalism

Personalism distinguishes 'between choices which are conceivably affected by the presence of the perceiver and choices which are not conceivably affected' (Jones and Davis, 1965). Naturally if one supposes that someone is doing something solely for one's benefit, one will not see it as typical. That is why a good interviewer will always look for confirmation of claims the interviewee makes about himself, particularly in reply to leads the interviewer himself gives.

### Perceived inability

This is a simple notion – for instance, if one knows that someone is very bad at tennis, one does not suppose that either his good shots or his losing the ball out of court are done deliberately.

### Non-common effects

This concept, by contrast, is difficult to grasp, at least initially, but is also one that has received a lot of attention. Actions have several effects, and the same person is usually seen performing several actions. A correspondent inference – about what someone meant to do, or what he is really like – is made on the basis of the 'non-common effects' of his actions. If someone chooses to go to Bournemouth, which has a sandy beach, a pier and a railway station, rather than Portsmouth, which has a pier, a railway station and a pebble beach, one might, for the moment ignoring all the other important differences between the two resorts, conclude that it was the sandy beach that mattered. It is the only 'non-common effect' of the choice. A pier and a railway station are common to both alternatives and so convey no information about the chooser's motives. It does not follow of course that the chooser does not care about piers or railway stations, rather that one would need information about his liking for other resorts that do not have piers or stations.

## Discounting effects

Any circumstance which leads the observer to suppose that an explanation of someone's behaviour as 'externally' or 'situationally' determined is more plausible is termed a 'discounting effect'. A man seen to do something because he is told to is not thought to have done it because he wants to. (But Karniol and Ross (1976) have shown that children under five don't think like this and see a child who was ordered or bribed to do something – both possible 'discounting effects' – as wanting to do it and liking doing it.) Koeske and Koeske (1975) showed that knowing a woman's menstrual period was due shortly made observers see moodiness as less of a sign of her personality than cheerfulness, because the moodiness could be 'discounted'. However, the 'discounting effect' of imminent menstruation was far from complete, and pre-menstrual moodiness still strongly coloured many observers' opinions of the woman's personality.

KELLEY'S ANALYSIS OF VARIANCE OR CUBE MODEL (ANOVA)

Jones and Davis's model is neither neat nor precise, whereas Kelley's ANOVA model, which starts with the consideration of common effects where Jones and Davis left off, is both (Kelley, 1967). Kelley's basic principle is that 'an effect is attributed to the one of its possible causes with which, over time, it co-varies'. One infers what it is someone is looking for in a seaside town, by observing where he goes and working out what appears to attract him and what appears not to. Similarly, if a man always treads on his partner's feet while dancing, regardless of who his partner is or what sort of dance they are doing, the logical conclusion is that he is clumsy. In Kelley's ANOVA model, this is known as 'person variance'. If, on the other hand, everyone always laughed at a particular comedian's jokes, including people who don't usually laugh much, the logical conclusion is that the comedian is funny. In Kelley's ANOVA model, this is known as 'entity variance'. Similarly, if the 'time' – the third side of Kelley's cube – determines behaviour, little is revealed about the person doing the act, or about the person receiving or reacting to it. Shaking hands with someone on meeting them reveals nothing about either person. This is known as 'occasion variance'. Finally, as Kelley points out, an action which is not typical of the person doing it, which is not typically associated with the person it is done to, and is not typical of the time and place, is not readily explained, except as 'bad luck'.

## The Theory viewed critically

Attribution theory in its various forms is not really a theory in the strict sense of the word; its authors say as much, describing it as 'an amorphous collection of observations about naïve causal inference' (Jones *et al.*, 1971). If attribution theory is not a theory, but is a model or a conceptual framework, then it must be judged by its usefulness and power to enlighten, rather than by its capacity to generate testable predictions. As a conceptual framework it fails to impress. Indeed much of the theory is remarkable for the vagueness and inelegance of its terminology. Consider, for example, this extract from Jones and Davis (1965): 'Given an attribute-effect linkage which is offered to explain why an act occurred, correspondence increases as the judged value of the attribute departs from the judge's conception of the average person's standing on that attribute.' This seems to mean that someone who sees another's behaviour as out-of-the-ordinarily dominant, will be particularly likely to explain it in terms of dominance. Scarcely a very profound thought.

In a sense of course, it is always circular and unhelpful to explain why someone does something by invoking a disposition or trait. Psychologists realized years ago that saying someone behaves politely because he is polite is not a proper explanation, even if the circularity is thinly disguised by phrases like 'politeness motive' or 'need to be polite'. Attribution theory's starting point is that people in general do talk and think in this circular way, but why? The theorists seem to have nothing to say on this point, having accepted Heider's (1958) argument that people and their intentions and dispositions are the 'givens' of 'common-sense psychology'. As Jones and Davis say, 'he eats because he is hungry' usually ends the discussion. (Unless, interestingly, the discussion includes a child, who will pursue an infinite regress of, why is he hungry? Why is his stomach empty? etc.) Why does common-sense psychology stop at a disposition? Is it because people don't know what causes hunger? Scarcely, for any intelligent schoolboy could talk about blood sugar levels and stomach contractions. Is it because 'hungry' is a sufficiently good explanation for most occasions? This may be true for hunger, but many dispositions, such as honesty, are not very good explanations, since they are arguably at too high a level of generality to mean anything concrete. Is it to end the discussion by putting someone in a pigeonhole, thereby also giving the perceiver the feeling that he understands, as Mischel (1968) and McHenry (1971) seem to be arguing? Attribution theory has said how and when traits are invoked as an explanation, but not why.

Another criticism of attribution theory is that it insists on a dichotomy between dispositions, traits and inner causes on the one hand, and the situation or outside causes on the other. This overlooks the fact that most behaviour is determined by a combination of both, and it unhelpfully lumps together all sorts of quite different factors because they are not inner dispositions. It may of course be argued that this is just what the naïve observer does, but then he is not given much choice in many of the reported experiments. Kelley, it is true, uses a three-way classification – person (inner dispositions), entity (other people, objects, attitudes, etc.) and times; this too is an oversimplification, and the 'entities' side of the cube covers a multitude of different things. Proof that Jones and Davis and Kelley oversimplify the way people see the reasons for behaviour comes from factor-analysis of 'locus-of-control' scales. These are intended to determine whether the person sees himself as controlling his life, or as being controlled by external circumstances. Levenson (1972) showed that subjects distinguished between external control by chance, and external control by powerful others, such as the Government. Collins (1974) found an even more complex picture, with no fewer than four types of external control being distinguished.

The link between the concepts in Jones and Davis's model and experimental manipulations is often very tenuous. For example, perceptions of the interviewee who acts out of role, in the experiment of

Jones *et al.* (1961), is laboriously explained as an example of 'non-common effects', because acting in role could be explained by a desire to avoid embarrassment, to gain approval from authority, and to manifest intelligence by showing understanding of the correct role of interviewee, etc. 'Hedonic relevance' is also a very general concept, meaning roughly that the action is gratifying or disappointing to the perceiver, and it is variously manipulated by requiring the subjects to express opinions they disagree with, making a group's reward contingent in a particular subject's performance, or causing subjects to think their efforts may win an exciting prize or a boring one. Concepts like 'non-common effects' or 'hedonic relevance' are so vague and general that virtually anything could be explained in terms of them.

## Attribution theory in action: some examples

DISTINCTIVENESS AND CONSENSUS INFORMATION

Theories are often most interesting when their predictions fail to work out – attribution theory is no exception. Jones and Davis argue that untypical behaviour is more revealing, while Kelley argues that behaviour everyone exhibits is uninformative, whereas 'distinctive' behaviour is not. This implies that being told everyone does something – consensus information – won't cause an observer to make dispositional inferences, whereas being told few people do – distinctiveness information – will. Miller *et al.* (1974) made ingenious use of the results of Milgram's (1963) well-known study of obedience to test this prediction. In Milgram's original study nearly all the subjects administered massive shocks to a not-very-willing victim (who was a confederate of the experimenter and never received the shocks). In Miller *et al.*'s study subjects were asked their opinion of someone who agreed to give such shocks, and were told either that most people agreed to give such shocks – consensus information – or were left to suppose, as most observers do, that few would. Subjects told what most people do in Milgram's experiment should see an individual willing shock-giver in a different light, as someone conforming to the demands of the experiment, not as someone with a nasty nature. They did not; they saw the shock-givers as being every bit as unpleasant as did the judges who were not told it was the usual response.

The failure of people to be influenced by consideration of what most people do is very consistent. Cooper, Jones and Tuller (1972) borrowed another standard experimental paradigm for their demonstration – the 'under-justified counter-attitudinal essay'. Subjects are led by the demands of the experiment to write an essay praising something they dislike and are given only 50 cents for doing so. Subsequently these subjects are found to have changed their opinion in the direction of that expressed in the essay, because, it is argued, they find this is the only way to justify having written it (whereas someone given a big enough bribe for writing the essay does not change their opinion as a result). Again, being told that most subjects agree to write the 'counter-attitudinal' essay should make it clear to observers that subjects were responding to the experimenter's demands, and should lead the observers to predict that the subjects won't change their opinions. This does not happen.

Nisbett *et al*. (1976) argue that people ignore information about how most people behave, simply because it is pallid and uninteresting – it is 'statistics'; they showed that the opinion of one person about a college course had more impact delivered informally and face-to-face, than the views of whole classes of students summarized in a survey of student opinion. Bertrand Russell (1927) had said it long before : 'Popular induction depends upon the emotional interest of the instances, not upon their number.'

Ross, Greene and House (1977) produced more data on an old theme, showing that people tend to expect others (the 'consensus') to act, think and feel like themselves. People who volunteer for an experiment expect others to do so too, people who support women's liberation expect others to follow suit, and people who are bad-tempered or frequently depressed tend to think others will feel the same. Ross *et al*. showed that this 'false consensus', unlike the real consensus, did work as Jones and Davis and Kelley argued it should; people who deviated from the perceiver's ideas about people in general were rated as more than usually shy, unadventurous, untrustworthy, etc. than the people who did not.

To return to a theme discussed in Chapter 2, man does not shine as an 'intuitive statistician', and many perceivers' ideas of 'what most people are like' seem readily confused with 'what a very few but near at hand and noticeable people are like' or with 'what I myself am like'.

## THE 'ACTOR-OBSERVER EFFECT'

Nisbett and Caputo, unpublished cited by Jones *et al*. (1971), gave the subjects in their experiment a very simple task and got a very interesting effect. Each subject was asked to write a paragraph explaining why he had chosen his degree course, and another explaining why he had chosen his girlfriend, then to explain the same choices as made by his best friend. Subjects tended to make 'stimulus attributions' – 'chemistry is a high-paying field' or 'she's a very warm person' – to explain their own choices, but 'person attributions' – 'he wants to earn a lot of money' or 'he likes warm girls' – when explaining their friends' choices. Inasmuch as 'he likes warm girls' and 'Mary (whom he likes) is a very warm girl' are very similar propositions, these findings might be regarded simply as facts of language; the same does not apply to the findings of Jones and Harris (1967). They found that observers thought someone believed what he was saying even when told he was reading from a script provided by the experimenter; they preferred to explain someone else's behaviour in terms of the person's character and outlook, not in terms of his response to outside pressures.

However, not all observers see the actor's reasons differently. An 'involved' observer – one who expects quite soon to be doing the same task as the person he is watching – sees that other person much as the person sees himself (Wolfson and Salancik, 1977), and the observer, instructed to empathize with the person he is observing, tends to see the person's behaviour as determined by outside forces. Perhaps the empathizing observer literally sees things the way the actor himself sees them. The actor does not see himself, he sees the things and people around him, so perhaps this is why he explains his behaviour as a response to these things and people, whereas the observer sees the actor, and sees him as the prime cause of what is happening. It is easy to change the actor's perspective by filming him, and when he watches himself, he sees his own behaviour more as a sign of an inner disposition (Storms, 1973). Similar results were obtained by placing the observers at different angles to the actors; the more visible the actor is, the more he is seen as causing what happens (Taylor and Fiske, 1975). It is even possible to increase the influence someone is seen as having on events by shining a brighter light on him (McArthur and Post, 1977).

However, Jones and Nisbett (1971) suggested another reason for the actor-observer effect, which is more profound than a simple change of perspective. They argued that the actor knows that his behaviour is a response to the situation, because he knows that he behaves differently at other times, in other places; the observer does not necessarily know this. The observer assumes that the actor is always like that, and furthermore, Jones and Nisbett argue, tends to rationalize inconsistencies in the actor's behaviour by invoking further traits, not by noticing that the circumstances have changed; thus, an apparently kind act by a person previously seen as hostile is seen as a sign that he is manipulative, condescending and insincere. This is, of course, an argument already developed in Chapter 2, and recurring in a slightly different form. If traits or dispositions are invoked to *explain away* behaviour, rather than explain it, it would follow that an observer will do this more often than the person himself. Monson and Snyder (1977) develop the theme that the actor knows best, and point out that subjects in psychology experiments are generally correct in seeing their behaviour as controlled by the experimenter, not by themselves. But the observer also is a subject in an experiment, so why doesn't he see the actor's behaviour as controlled by the experimenter, as he knows his own is? Monson and Snyder argue that often the observer is not told what led up to the behaviour he is observing and evaluating, so he does not know what part the experimenter has played in causing it.

A further difficulty for Jones and Nisbett is that people don't see the behaviour of close friends any differently from that of distant acquaintances or public figures. On Jones and Nisbett's hypothesis, they should, for they have more opportunity to realize that the behaviour of close friends is not highly consistent and predictable, and not necessarily the product of a few monolithic personality traits. The original study of Nisbett and Caputo (cited in Jones *et al*., 1971) asked subjects about themselves and their best friends, which in the light of Nisbett's later theorizing was not the best comparison to make. Nisbett *et al* (1973) compared the number of traits attributed by subjects to themselves, their fathers, their best friends, admired acquaintances, and a distant public figure (Walter Cronkite). The actor-observer effect was found, but no effect of the degree of acquaintance emerged. Nor could Taylor and Koivumaki (1976) find any evidence that people saw their spouse's behaviour as, like their own, caused by events, not by dispositions. Actually, in the light of some of some of the research on the accuracy with which husbands and wives see each other's point of view, discussed in Chapter 8, these results are not that surprising. Long and close acquaintance with someone does not necessarily help one see their behaviour, thoughts or feeling with any special degree of clarity.

WHO'S TO BLAME?

Piaget had discussed the way children assign guilt and responsibility long before the advent of attribution theory, and had made the interesting observation that children tend to judge an action by its consequences, rather than by the intention that produced it; thus, to a child, breaking six cups by accident is worse than breaking one on purpose. It has been suggested that the idea of things happening by accident at all is alien, not just to children, but to whole sections of humanity, who explain all natural events as caused by supernatural agencies; the sun sets because it wants to and rain falls because the rain god is pleased, and does not if he is angry (Maselli and Altrocchi, 1969).

Walster (1966) started a long and complicated argument when she presented evidence showing that American adults also tend to think in this primitive and irrational way. Her experimental subjects were given the history of a teenage boy who left his elderly and somewhat decrepit car parked on a steep hill, down which is subsequently rolled, causing either a lot of damage or very little, to itself or to other people and other cars. The more damage that was caused, the more responsible the owner of the car was held to be for the accident.

This result, which was consistent with Piaget's description of children's moral judgements, and with some sorts of common sense, was soon challenged by a series of contradictory or negative findings. Walster herself (1967) showed that a person who bought a new house and lost money on it, through a landslide or because an expected job fell through, was not judged the more responsible for his loss, the bigger it was. Indeed in one part of the study the man who lost a lot was actually seen as less to blame for his loss. Other failures to replicate the 1966 finding include the studies of Shaver (1970), Shaw and Skolnick (1971) as well as several unpublished studies. Of these failures to replicate, only one of Shaver's (1970) three studies is an actual repeat of Walster's 1966 study, and its failure to find the same as Walster could be explained by small sample sizes (only 8 subjects in one condition) and the admitted inability of some of the subjects to understand their task.

Some order has been imposed on the chaos, by the discovery that similarity between the person judging responsibility and the person suffering the consequences generally results in the victim being seen as less to blame for his misfortune (McKillip and Posavac, 1972), although Shaw and Skolnick found the opposite, males judging males more harshly. Similarly it has been suggested that Walster (1967) failed to find an effect because her student subjects did not feel involved in the fate of older, house-purchasing others. Chaikin and Darley (1973) found that the more serious the accident, the more likely it was to be judged to be someone's fault; however, the subject's choice of who to blame depended on the role the subject expected to play in the experiment.

Much of the confusion of the results undoubtedly arises from the variety of experimental stories used, some of which obviously are likely to be quite different in their effects. In Walster's (1967) house-buying experiment the mild or serious consequences are quite beyond the control of the buyer, being an act of God, or an act of the US Government. Chaikin and Darley used a videotaped presentation of a 'supervisor' 'accidentally' knocking over a 'worker's' pile of bricks, with severity of outcome being manipulated by telling the observers that the 'worker' either automatically lost pay as a result of the 'supervisor's' clumsiness, or didn't. Quite a few studies by contrast have used Walster's original (1966) material, or a variation involving an accident to a child visiting a factory on an open day. Here the subject's ideas about blame are likely to be conditioned by the law, which in practice, if not in principle, often assigns more responsibility to the supervisor, the worse the effect of an action happens to be. A man whose car rolls down a hill but causes only minor damage to itself would be unlucky to suffer legal consequences, whereas someone – without insurance – whose car – with its possibly defective brakes – rolled down a hill, demolished a shop, and seriously injured the shop-keeper, would be remarkably lucky to avoid both civil and criminal prosecution. Similarly, safety at work is the subject of many laws, all of which tend to place a heavy burden of responsibility on management and workers. A few offences are subject to 'absolute liability', which means that the prosecution don't have to prove intent, merely that the action was performed, and had an effect. Certainly, in practice, the more serious the effects of an accident, the more attention will be paid to it, and the more likely it is that breaches of the law, such as no insurance or defective brakes, will come to light. Perhaps the irrationality lies not in holding someone responsible for carelessly causing a serious accident, but in not bothering to hold them responsible for carelessness that happens not to cause an accident.

The research considered so far has had as its focus of concern the person who caused or occasioned the accident, but what of the victim – the child injured by the factory accident, or the grocer in his shop at the bottom of Walster's hill? One would assume naturally that the experimental subjects would feel sympathy for the child. The research of Lerner and his assistants showed that this may not be the case. Lerner (1965) originally found that observers persuaded themselves that the subject who was rewarded for his work was a better worker, even though they were clearly told the worker to be rewarded was chosen by lot. Lerner and Simmons (1966) went on to show that the subject who was punished with electric shocks – again as a result, ostensibly, of a drawing of lots – was seen as less attractive, and less likely to be popular. Lerner developed the idea of the 'belief in a just world' to explain these effects, arguing that observers expect an orderly and fair relationship between what people do and what happens to them, an expectation that is upset when people get rewarded or punished at random. Observers protect their belief by persuading themselves that rewards and punishments were not random, but have been earned, in some unspecified fashion, by the people who receive them. Lerner and Simmons developed their theme by showing that rejection of the shock victim is greater when the programme of punishment is scheduled to continue than when it is over, because, it is argued, a continuing injustice is a bigger affront to the belief in a just world than one that has ceased. Rejection is greatest when the victim is a 'martyr', someone who didn't really want to get electric shocks, but who agreed reluctantly so that the subjects themselves should not lose their opportunity to do the experiment and gain a course credit.

Rubin and Peplau (1975) developed an attitude scale of 'belief in a just world', and found that people who clung to such a belief tended to be more religious and more authoritarian, which led to the suggestion that it represents a primitive, child-like way of observing things.

Those who find Lerner's results unpalatable can take some comfort from the recent paper of Godfrey and Lowe (1975) who argued that they can be explained in terms of the person/situation distinction of attribution theory. The rejected victims in Lerner's research were seen as responding to outside pressures to participate in experiments that deprived them of choice, or were seen as being easily bullied by the experimenter into doing something they didn't want to do, which is why they were rejected. Subjects seen to volunteer to take electric shocks for a worthwhile scientific purpose were not rated unfavourably.

In fact, Piaget's ideas about perceived responsibility, and Heider's which developed from them (Heider, 1958), are more complex than a simple distinction between blame and innocence. Heider distinguishes five levels of responsibility, which Shaw and Sulzer (1964) investigated in a survey of adults and children. At level one, Global-Association, being anywhere near or in any way connected with the act means that one is guilty, so that a child whose toy gun is used by another child to hit someone would be seen responsible for the injury. Few children, aged 6 to 9, or adults actually thought like this. The second level, Extended Commission, covers unforseeable consequences of acts, such as startling someone by knocking on their door and causing them to drop something: as Piaget predicted, children are more likely than adults to see the actor as responsible for such accidents. At level three, Careless Commission, the person is responsible, through carelessness, for what happens, while at level four, Purposive Commission, he is responsible in the full usual sense. Children and adults don't differ in their judgement at these levels, but both distinguish between the careless and deliberate commission of acts leading to good or bad results; both children and adults consider people more responsible when their actions cause injury or loss. (This finding confirms Walster's (1966) finding; Fishbein and Ajzen (1973) suggest that the confusing findings of subsequent research results from condensing Heider's five levels to only two.)

The fifth level is Justified Commission, where a deliberate act might still be excused as being done under duress; in fact neither children nor adults did give any credit, in the shape of lesser ratings of responsibility, for acting under someone else's control, especially when the outcome was bad. Shaw and Sulzer's intentional, but possibly justified actions, were fairly trivial, such as a boy making a good job of mowing a lawn when told to by his mother. It is not difficult to think of other cases where acting on orders would be quite likely to be accepted as an excuse; for example, if the person giving the orders were an armed criminal. But here again 'acting on orders' is not always accepted as an excuse, even when the penalty for disobedience could be death; 'acting on orders' was specifically rejected by the winning side in the Second World War as an excuse for the losing side's inhuman actions (just as it almost certainly would have been rejected by the other side, had they won, as excusing, for example, the bombing of civilian targets).

Research so far has scarcely begun to unravel the complexities of assigning responsibility for actions, and would probably make faster progress if a more complex model, even than Heider's five levels of responsibility and two levels of outcome, could be developed. In particular, the role of the law in shaping people's ideas about responsibility needs to be considered, as well, of course, as the more profound question of how the law itself came to be shaped.

GIVING CREDIT WHERE CREDIT'S DUE

If things go badly wrong, people tend to look around for someone to blame, but if they work out well what determines who gets the credit? An early experiment by Johnson, Feigenbaum and Weib (1964) seemed to show that people took the credit if things go well, but blamed others if they went badly. Trainee educational psychologists tried to teach simple arithmetic to two pupils, one of whom got his sums right and one of whom did not. The trainees attributed the successful pupil's success to their own skill as a teacher, but explained the other pupil's failure as proof that he was stupid, lazy or both. Beckman (1970) obtained similar results; an improving performance was proof of the teacher's skill, whereas deteriorating performance, over a series of four sessions, showed that the pupil was not trying. The same sort of result emerges when people are doing a difficult task, such as solving a series of anagrams, or being tested for social perceptiveness, and find that they do consistently well, or consistently badly, or get better with practice, or get worse. In the anagram experiments, e.g. Feather (1969) the anagrams actually vary in difficulty, whereas in the social perception experiments, e.g. Davis and Davis (1972), the task is so vague that the subjects can equally plausibly be told they have done well or done badly, regardless of their actual replies.

Subsequent research, e.g. Luginbuhl, Crowe and Kahan (1975), had distinguished between two 'internal' factors – 'effort', which is variable, and 'ability', which is constant, as well as between two 'external' factors – the 'difficulty' of the task, which is constant, and 'luck', which is variable. Luginbuhl et al. found that people who succeeded modestly attributed their success to effort rather than ability, whereas people who 'failed' tended to say the task was difficult – actually it was impossible – and that they lacked ability.

The idea that people don't see the causes of their own successes and failures dispassionately seems so immediately compelling, especially to anyone who has discussed a football match with a player from the losing side, that it comes as something of a surprise to find it challenged. Miller and Ross (1975) argue that subjects in experiments like that of Johnson *et al*. are doing their best to draw conclusions from the evidence at their disposal and are not thinking irrationally. For example if *one* of the teacher's two pupils does get his sums right, the teacher can reasonably assume that he has some teaching ability, so that the only reasonable explanation for the other pupil's failure must lie with the pupil. On the same reasoning Luginbuhl *et al*.'s subjects are quite rational too; a task on which one performs poorly is likely to be difficult, because sensible experimenters do not give their subjects impossible tasks to do.

However, several recent studies have produced definite evidence of defensive bias in the way people see their successes and failures. Nicholls (1975) caused his subjects to succeed twice, to fail twice, to fail first then succeed, or to succeed first then fail, and then asked them to assess the respective contributions of ability, effort, luck and task difficulty to their performance. Subjects whose performance was consistent had more grounds for attributing their performance to their ability, or lack of it, than subjects whose performance varied from one trial to another, and rationally enough, the double success and double failure subjects saw ability as more important than the other two groups, but when it came to assessing the role luck played, evidence of bias emerged. Subjects who failed twice saw themselves as influenced by luck just as much as did the subject who failed once, but the subjects who succeeded twice didn't think luck came into it much, giving it only 5 per cent of the credit for their performance. If bad luck accounts for consistent failure, shouldn't good luck account for consistent success?

Arkin, Gleason and Johnston (1976) allowed half their subjects to choose which of a number of courses of therapy to give, but randomly assigned the other half to a treatment-giving group. The treatments either 'worked', apparently making an anxious person more relaxed, or didn't. The subjects who were assigned to give a treatment might be expected to feel less responsible for its success or failure, than ones who chose a treatment, but in practice subjects took the credit if the treatment worked, even if it had been assigned to them, but dissociated themselves if it didn't – 'heads I win, tails you lose'.

The final line of evidence on defensive bias comes from two studies on sex-role expectations, by Feldman-Summers and Kiesler (1974). When male and female students assessed the role of ability, effort, difficulty, and luck in causing other male and female students to succeed and fail, all subjects, in all conditions, saw the women as making more effort, perhaps because, as the experimenters argue, subjects thought that to do as well as the men, women had to try harder. The second study showed that men thought women succeeded in medicine through effort, while men succeed more by ability; women judges agreed with the men about the role of effort but not about that of ability.

## SELF-ATTRIBUTION

Attribution theorists claim that people explain others' actions as caused by a shifting combination of internal and external causes; 'self-attribution' theory argues that people explain their own behaviour in the same way. If external causes seem sufficient to explain one's behaviour, then one will see it as caused by them, but if they don't seem sufficient, one will conclude that one's behaviour is internally caused, which is a clumsy way of saying that one will see it as intentional or deliberate. The point is that the person doesn't have any special insight into his actions or his reasons for them, but tends rather to judge himself in the same way he would judge someone else.

Bem (1972) explains the results of Festinger and Carlsmith's (1959) well-known insufficient reward experiment in self-attribution terms. The subjects of this study performed a very boring task for a while, before being persuaded by the experimenter to tell the next subject that the task was really very interesting. They were given $1 or $20 to tell this lie, and were then asked again for their own opinion of the task. The heavily bribed $20 subjects still thought it was very boring, but the $1 group now thought it was more interesting. Festinger explained this result by invoking a motivational state called 'cognitive dissonance' – the awareness of an inconsistency between thought and thought or between thought and action creates a pressure, most easily relieved for the $1 subjects by changing their opinion of the task. Bem argues that it is unnecessary to bring in subjective pressures and states, and asks what outside observers would make of the $1 and $20 subjects? A person who tells someone something is likely to be telling the truth, unless there is some obvious reason for him to lie, such as a $20 bribe. Perhaps the subject sees himself as others see him; he usually means what he says, unless he knows that he has a good reason – such as $20 – not to.

This interesting theme has been elaborated in a number of ways. Bem has demonstrated that observers, given the scripts of experiments like that of Festinger and Carlsmith, made the same choices as the subjects in the original experiments, which is consistent with the hypothesis that the person sees his own behaviour as others see it. A series of experiments on motivation (Deci, 1971) showed that people offered money, an 'extrinsic' reward, to do something they find interesting, or 'intrinsically' rewarding, tend to 'discount' dispositional factors as explaining their own behaviour. In plain English, paying someone to do something they like doing anyway makes it less interesting and enjoyable. Mark Twain's Tom Sawyer took the argument a step farther; something you pay for the privilege of doing, like whitewashing a fence, stops being a chore and becomes fun. As Staw (1976) notes, the findings of research like Deci's have obvious implications for industry.

## ATTRIBUTION THERAPY?

Self-attribution theory has other possible practical implications as well. An early study by Valins (1966) showed that it is possible to lead men to prefer certain pin-ups, by causing a tape-recorded heart beat to speed up or slow down, when they were presented. The subjects thought the sound was of their own heart, and inferred from its change of rate that the accompanying pin-up was more exciting. Later research (Hirshman, 1975) has extended the effect to unpleasant pictures of people who had died violent deaths, and showed that falsely telling the subject that his heart was beating faster produced a real increase in his 'electro-dermal activity'.[1] However, Taylor (1975) argues that the 'Valins Effect' only works where the subject's preferences are fairly unimportant to him, so it would not be possible to convince someone that they did not like a close friend, or did like an enemy. In Taylor's experiment subjects' preferences could only be manipulated by 'false feedback' about heart rate, when the subject didn't expect ever to meet the people depicted; if they thought they were selecting partners for the next phase of the experiment, changes in their supposed heart rate didn't influence their choice.

If Taylor's argument is correct, 're-attribution' caused by false

---

[1] A new name for an old phenomenon – the changes in the skin preparatory to sweating, taken as an index of tension or arousal.

feedback can never have much practical application, because it could never affect behaviour that mattered to the person. Valins and Ray (1967) had earlier succeeded in changing behaviour, but not attitudes, by false feedback; people previously afraid of snakes were willing to approach them more closely after being given false feedback that their heart rate didn't change at the sight of a snake. They still said they were frightened of snakes. Storms and Nisbett (1970) took the possibilities of 'attribution therapy' a stage further. Instead of telling the subject he was excited when he wasn't, or wasn't excited when he was, they told their subjects they were indeed excited, but not for the reason they thought. Their subjects were people who could not sleep at night, and the treatment took the seemingly odd and even self-defeating form of giving them a pill to take before going to bed, which it was said would increase their heart rate, raise their temperature, and send thoughts racing through their minds. In fact, the pill was inert and had no physical effect at all. Storms and Nisbett argued that the sleepless subjects would attribute their usual bedtime symptoms of high pulse and temperature, and racing thoughts to the pill, not to insomnia, would not worry about not being able to sleep and would consequently fall alseep sooner. In Storms and Nisbett's experiment, insomniacs given the bogus pill that was supposed to cause tension did fall asleep on average twelve minutes sooner than they had previously.

A similarly ingenious experiment has been reported by Dienstbier and Munter (1971), in which students 'failed' a particularly important test, after being given an inert pill that was supposed to increase heart rate, make the palms sweat, and give a sinking feeling in the pit of the stomach. It was made very easy for the students to cheat, after they'd 'failed', and to raise their score above the pass mark. Of the males who'd had the allegedly tension-producing pill, 56 percent did cheat, as opposed to only 17 percent of the control group, whose pill was supposed to make them sleepy. Dienstbier and Munter's explanation was that all subjects felt tense at the idea of cheating after their 'failure', but the ones who'd had the supposed tension-producing pill attributed their feelings to the pill, and not to anxiety. Not feeling anxiety at the thought of cheating made it easy for them to do just that – cheat.

Some of these 're-attribution' effects aren't easy to obtain however. Dienstbier and Munter's female subjects didn't cheat more under the influence of the supposed drug, and Storms and Nisbett's insomnia cure hasn't always worked (e.g. Kellogg and Baron, 1975). Many people have doubts about giving their subjects or patients bogus pills or false information about their heart rate, and it's arguable that a form of treatment based on deliberately lying to the patient could never have much of a future. Fortunately, it's possible to use methods derived from attribution theory, to change people's behaviour, without telling them more than a few small white lies. Miller, Brickman and Bolen (1975) found that a school class could be made to keep their classroom free of litter, by telling them at frequent intervals how tidy they *were* – which they weren't in fact – and that this worked a great deal better than telling them how tidy they *ought to be*. The effect lasted at least two weeks. Miller *et al.*'s second experiment, using the same technique, succeeded in producing a slight but significant and lasting improvement on a series of maths tests.

CONCLUSIONS

Attribution theory has, if nothing else, stimulated research on person perception in general, and on the interpretation of behaviour in particular. It had previously been something of a failing of person perception research that it concentrated too narrowly on particular parts of its subject matter, such as facial expressions of emotion, or ratings of personality traits, and had neglected the way people perceive behaviour itself. Attribution theory has posed some interesting questions, even if it hasn't answered many of them. In particular, the curious difference in the way people judge and describe their own behaviour and that of others deserves more study. Other lines of research have been less promising; the research on consensus and distinctiveness finally rediscovers the assumed similarity effect, that people expect others to react like them, while the research on attribution therapy seems hard to replicate. Research in other fields, notably the attribution of responsibility, is interesting but needs conceptual clarification urgently. This, to a greater or lesser extent, applies to the whole theory, which is so loose and vague, as hardly to merit the name 'theory'.

# 6 IMPLICIT PERSONALITY THEORIES
## Inferences from inferences

> He behaved just as I should have expected a great, fat,
> self-indulgent man to behave under trying circumstances
> – that is to say very badly.
>
> From *The Truth about Pyecraft* by
> H.G. Wells

In terms of the model of person perception outlined in Chapters 2 and 3, Wells has an implicit personality theory (IPT) that fat, self-indulgent people behave very badly in trying circumstances. Wells's IPT has a number of typical features; he infers from visible superficial characteristics – 'fat'; he uses more than one piece of information – 'great, fat, self-indulgent'; and he infers from one personality trait to another – 'self-indulgent'; he is also markedly censorious in tone – 'behaved very badly'. These various features of implicit personality theories are discussed in this and the two previous chapters; this chapter will be concerned with the way traits are seen as going together, and with the way such groups of traits often carry a value judgement with them. The role of visible characteristics, such as fatness, or Englishness, was discussed in Chapter 4 and the way people make inferences from behaviour was discussed in Chapter 5. Although logically related, the research on these three issues has been done within somewhat different traditions, using markedly different methods; research on the way people infer traits from other traits has perhaps the longest and most diverse history.

HISTORICAL BACKGROUND

Before the Second World War, when the hope that psychology would advance as fast and as far as physics or chemistry was as yet undimmed, scientific rating schedules were very popular in American industrial and educational psychology (but never caught on in Britain). The supervisor or teacher had to rate the workers or pupils on an interminable list of qualities, ranging from 'teachability' through 'public relations' to 'monetary responsibility' (a scale for insurance salesmen), or from 'is he negativistic or suggestible' to 'is he even tempered or moody' (the Haggarty-Olson-Wickman Schedules for rating children). Enthusiasm for rating schedules of this type was reduced by the discovery that the two dozen or four dozen or 101 ratings the rater produced were not independent; they were more likely to represent no more than two or three separate judgements, possibly only one. The worker who was rated as punctual, was also rated as keen, competent, well-disciplined, likeable, popular and polite, just as the pupil who was good at his work was also quiet, popular and well-adjusted. Are people really that consistent? or does the fault lie in the rater's judgement? Almost certainly it is the latter. The tendency to give consistently good ratings to the people the rater liked or approved of was called the 'halo effect'. The related but opposite tendency, to give consistently poor ratings to unpopular people has occasionally been called the 'horns effect'. The assumption that that traits go together when in fact they do not has been called 'logical error'.

When the study of IPTs originated, they were seen simply as one of the many disadvantages of rating scales; however, it was soon realized that there was more to them than that, and that they determined the way people see each other all the time, not just when completing rating scales. Thus, they came to be regarded as an important topic of research in social psychology, and also as a personality variable under the name of 'cognitive complexity'. Eventually, at least two major approaches to personality emphasized the point that people respond to what they see, not to what is actually there, and that the most important thing they see is other people; therefore, in the eyes of Blake and Ramsey (1951), and later of Kelly (1955), the way people see each other is the most important topic in psychology.

All these considerations, and the central role of IPTs in person perception, point to the importance of studying them.

## Methods of uncovering implicit personality theories

An 'implicit personality theory' is what is says – 'implicit'; the man in the street doesn't necessarily know that he expects fat, self-indulgent people to behave badly, so when attempting to discover what views about other people someone less articulate than H.G. Wells has, a degree of subtlety is required. Three basic methods, may be distinguished, in order of sophistication: ratings, co-occurrence, and the Role Repertory Grid Test.

## RATINGS

There are many rating formats; the ones used most often are the 'cue trait' method, devised by Bruner, Shapiro and Taguiri (1958) and the 'semantic differential' devised by Osgood *et al.* (1957). The cue trait method employs this format:

A person is *warm*.     How likely is he to be:
generous      — — — — — — —      stingy?
intelligent    — — — — — — —      unintelligent?
etc.

The semantic differential makes the purpose of the task a little less obvious, with this format:

|  | Your best friend |  |
|---|---|---|
| soft   — — — — — — — | hard |
| warm   — — — — — — — | cold |
| nice   — — — — — — — | nasty |
| slow   — — — — — — — | fast |

Correlation, factor analysis and more elaborate statistical techniques are used to determine which traits are seen as belonging together. A three-dimensional structure usually emerges, with 'evaluation' the largest dimension, underlying the most scales, followed by 'potency' and 'activity'. 'Potency' is defined by adjectives like 'strong', 'hard', or 'masculine', while 'activity' is defined by ones like 'fast', 'bright' and of course 'active'.

## CO-OCCURRENCE

This technique, used by Rosenberg and Sedlak (1972) in their research, is derived from free description; each person is asked to describe several others by sorting trait names into different groups, each group representing a different person. (Alternatively the data can be obtained from literary extracts like Wells's description of Pyecraft; Rosenberg and Jones (1972) have published an analysis of the American writer Theodore Dreiser's implicit personality theory, as revealed in his novel *A Gallery of Women*.) If Rosenberg's subjects consistently use a pair of trait names, such as 'sociable' and 'intelligent' to describe the same person, these words are taken as having something in common. This basically simple idea becomes complicated when every paired combination of eighty or ninety-nine traits has to be analysed and a statistical technique called 'multidimensional scaling' is employed. An analysis of personality traits used by American college students is illustrated in Figure 6.1; the nearer two words are, the more similarly they are used, so that 'easygoing' and 'intelligent' are used to describe the same people, whereas 'polite' and 'intelligent' are not.

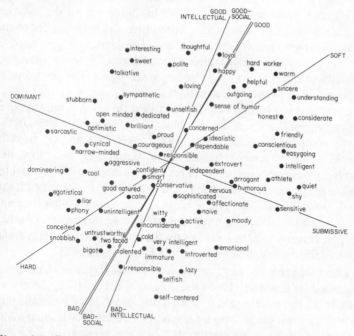

*Figure* 6.1   Rosenberg and Sedlak's (1972) data on similarity of meaning of trait names, determined by 'co-occurrence'. The dimensions 'good/bad' etc. are derived from ratings made of the traits and factor–analysed.

Rosenberg's method, like the rating method, generally uses group data – Figure 6.1 summarizes the data from fifty men and fifty women; critics, like Allport (1937) point out that it is quite possible for an average IPT not to correspond to every, most, or conceivably any individual theory. While it is quite possible to analyse individual theories by rating or co-occurrence methods, as Rosenberg and Jones did for Theodore Dreiser, the analysis of individual IPTs more often uses the most elaborate method, conceptually similar to Rosenberg's technique – the Role Repertory Grid Test.

## ROLE REPERTORY GRID TEST

This method, devised by Kelly (1955), is illustrated in Figure 6.2. The subject first fills in the initials of actual people corresponding to the roles that make up the twenty 'elements'. He 'generates' his first 'construct' by considering three elements, deciding which two differ from the third, and putting a name to the distinction. In the example in Figure 6.2, the subject himself and his father are 'strong', and his mother is 'weak'. The same distinction then has to be applied to the other seventeen role figures. The second 'construct' is generated in the same way, except that a different triad of role figures are used, and the subject is forbidden to use 'strong/weak' again. The procedure is repeated until twenty 'constructs' have been generated, after which the 'grid', as it is usually called, is analysed, to discern, among other things, which characteristics the subject sees as going together. In the partly completed example of Figure 6.2 it can be seen that, broadly speaking, everyone who is 'strong' is also 'determined' and 'firm', but rarely 'female' or 'unreliable'. This subject has an IPT that strong people are firm, determined and reliable, and can be identified fairly easily by their sex. The 'grid' usually reveals a large evaluative component, a halo effect in the way the person completing it sees other people. It tends to reveal also, as do the other methods, that people have relatively few independent ways of seeing others.

There are many different versions of the Role Repertory Grid Test, described by Bonarius (1965) and Adams-Webber (1970); later versions of the test have tended to make it shorter and more artificial. The subject does not use his own words to describe his classifications, but makes use of 'provided constructs'. In some versions he does not judge real people he knows, but is provided with photographs of strangers. These shorter, standardized versions take less time to

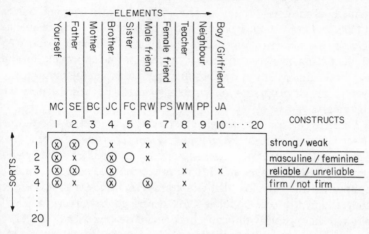

*Figure* 6.2 Part of a completed Role Repertory Grid. The circles indicate which three elements or role figures are considered first, and generate the construct for that sort.

complete and are easier to score, but lose the two main virtues of the original – that the object of the exercise is not made too obvious to the subject, and that he is allowed to use his own words.

## Types of implicit personality theory

### VARIATIONS IN THE CHOICE OF COMPONENT TERMS

Little (1969) using the Repertory Grid found that women make more use of personality and interpersonal terms in describing others, whereas men describe others more in terms of role, achievement and physical characteristics. The attributes people mention also vary according to their age, and the proportion of psychological terms used increases from the age of thirteen or fourteen. Adolescent girls tend to describe others in terms of their physical appearance to a great extent, forming an exception to the general rule that women talk less in physical terms and more in psychological terms. In Rosenberg and Sedlak's (1972) research, the single word the subjects most frequently used to describe each other was 'intelligent', which is not all that surprising since they were psychology students. Rosenberg and Sedlak found two dimensions underlying the judgement their subjects made of each other – the familiar warm/cold dimension, and one of intellectual evaluation. Friendly and Glucksberg (1970) were able to identify the same two dimensions in the slang of Princeton students; student slang changes almost year by year, so the appearance of the two basic dimensions in it shows they are more than the remains of a way of seeing people no longer actually used, but fossilized in the dictionary.

Crockett (1965) has summarized several studies using a free description measure of the number of concepts that subjects use. Study of the number of concepts used to describe liked and disliked people of differing ages and different sex produced complex results, supporting the principle that people have more ideas about people they frequently see. Nidorf (1961, described by Crockett, 1965) showed that people with many concepts for dealing with others were better able to integrate conflicting information about another person; a person who sees others only in terms of whether they share his political opinions is unlikely to be able to come to terms with the idea of someone who has all sorts of desirable qualities, but who is opposed to him in political ideology.

## BROAD DIMENSIONS UNDERLYING IMPLICIT PERSONALITY THEORIES

People use many different words to describe others, but they do not use them independently. People expect one attribute to be associated with another – the 'logical error' and the 'halo effect'. These groupings of attributes can be very broad, so that a dozen or more terms will all be used in the same way. This research has mostly used the cue trait and semantic differential methods, which produce similar results: three or five or six group factors. (The Repertory Grid yields, more laboriously, the same pattern.) The semantic differential factors, first extracted by Osgood *et al.* (1957), are called 'evaluation', 'potency' and 'activity'. A later study by Lay and Jackson (1969), using the cue trait method, also found three factors: aggression/social desirability, compulsivity/control and independence/dependence. Three similar factors have been extracted from ratings of facial expressions: pleasant/unpleasant, attention/rejection and degree of activation (Schlosberg, 1954). However, analysis of ratings of people or facial expressions does not always produce three dimensions. Warr and Haycock (1970) found six factors with an English sample: *two* evaluation factors, *two* activity factors and *two* potency factors.

Most studies have chosen trait names more or less at random; Cattell (1946) argued that analysis should proceed more systematically. He started with Allport and Odbert's (1936) list of 17,953 trait names, eliminated obsolete and marginally relevant terms, and grouped the remainder in 171 clusters. These were then further reduced to thirty-six clusters, dubbed the 'standard reduced personality sphere'. A study by Norman (1963) factor analysed ratings on the thirty-six clusters, and found five factors. (The variation in number of factors found in analyses of similar rating data often puzzles people. It arises for two reasons. In the first place some methods of analysis look for a larger number of correlated factors, e.g. sixteen, which can be further factor analysed to yield two or three 'second-order factors'. Secondly, the smaller factors extracted after the larger first factors are often statistically unreliable.)

## Real or perceived personality?

Three factors – evaluation ('good/bad'), activity ('active/passive'), and potency ('strong/weak') – or something fairly similar emerge from most studies, but what do they signify? Early researchers, and later personality theorists like Cattell, take them as a representation of the actual structure of human personality; in other words people can be placed on real dimensions of good/bad, weak/strong, and active/passive, however named. The other view, that the factors, represent linguistic or cognitive structures in the mind of the rater, is supported by the work of Mulaik (1964) and Passini and Norman (1966); they found the same structure of three factors in ratings of strangers or stereotyped figures, whose real personality structure would either be unknown to the raters, or non-existent. (How can 'a liked person' have a personality?) On the other hand Lay and Jackson (1969) showed that the same three factor structure emerged from factor analysis of a personality questionnaire, the Personality Research Form, in which the subjects give answers like 'I spend a lot of time visiting friends'. This implies either that the three factors are really aspects of personality after all, or that their influence over the perceiver's conceptual system is so pervasive as to affect the way he answers questions about his own behaviour, as well as the way he rates other people. Similarly, Stricker, Jacobs and Kogan (1974) found that when people sorted out items from the MMPI Psychopathic Deviance (Pd) scale, according to their apparent similarity, they tended to reproduce the factors of the scale. Stricker *et al*. take this as evidence that judgements correspond to the true structure of personality, as measured by the test, but it could just as well be taken to show the opposite – that personality structures measured by questionnaire reflect, like those measured by ratings, the way people see each other, rather than the way they really are.

It is unlikely, as Fiske (1974) points out, that the issue can be resolved, until the study of personality disentangles itself from the study of person perception, by finding measures of individual differences that do not rely on the judgement of observers who use everyday concepts of human behaviour and character.

### The problem of the halo

Those who think rating factors exist in the personality of the rated, rather than in the eye of the rater, also have to explain why the largest factor is always a value judgement. How can 'good/bad' be a true personality trait? When someone who is rated 'good' is also 'clean and warm and bright', is it not obvious that 'clean', 'warm' and 'bright' are not being used literally, but metaphorically? They express generally desirable qualities, rather than point to an absence of dirt, shivering or stupidity. In many studies, the raters have no choice because they are not rating a real person and cannot know if he is literally clean, warm or bright.

Several attempts have been made to prove that ratings of people need not be largely evaluative. Kuusinen (1969) took the bold step of statistically eliminating the evaluation, potency and activity factors and found six purely descriptive factors, all about the same size, which he identified as honesty, rationality, self-confidence, unpredictability, tolerance and sociability. Miron (1969) dismissed this as a statistical trick and said the six descriptive factors were chance effects that would not emerge from a replication. Peabody (1967) noted that the semantic differential method confounds evaluation and description, because the scale labels are usually only half of a set of four adjectives. Thus the scale 'timid/bold' uses the pejorative term 'timid' for one pole (and not the approving term 'cautious') and the approving term 'bold' for the other (and not the pejorative term 'rash'). Peabody's data seemed to show that when the rater is given evaluatively balanced scales, e.g. 'cautious/bold' or 'timid/rash', his ratings are less influenced by evaluation. A later paper by Rosenberg and Olshan (1970) pointed out errors in Peabody's statistics, which, when corrected, restored the evaluative factor. It appears that a liking for someone does exercise a pervasive influence over ratings made of them.

## Cognitive complexity and individual differences in implicit personality theories

While research on the broad dimensions underlying the average IPT generally uses group data, often from very large samples, and obtained by rating methods, research on individual differences in the way people see each other's personalities tends to use the more elaborate and sensitive Repertory Grid methods. A main focus of interest has been the differences between people who have a lot of independent concepts and those who have few. Someone who has only one concept for dealing with other people – a recorded example is 'in the US Army/not in the US Army' – is likely to differ in important ways from someone who has up to half a dozen independent concepts, such as the list – social skill, intelligence, motivation, personal stability, experience – often recommended to selection interviewers. This dimension is often called 'cognitive complexity', but there is some confusion about the term. Crockett (1965) uses it to refer to the overall number of concepts used by the subject, regardless of whether they were used in the same way or not, and to the number of independent concepts; he suggested that the two measures were highly correlated. Little (1969) shows that they are in fact completely uncorrelated. Bieri (1966) draws a useful distinction, between the number of independent dimensions the person employs – which he calls 'differentiation' – and the number of points along a particular dimension the person discriminates – 'articulation'. Bieri's 'differentiation' corresponds to the commonly accepted definition of cognitive complexity: the number of *independent* dimensions.

A number of findings emerge from research on cognitive complexity (Crockett, 1965). Extroverts and members of college fraternities are more complex. Women are more complex. Less complex judges see others in 'black and white' terms and also tend to think that social relations are more neat and 'balanced' than they really are. There is some evidence that complex people can integrate conflicting information about others, although this has not always been replicated. There is no relation between intelligence and cognitive complexity. Less complex judges assume similarity to a greater extent, but are not less accurate than more complex judges. Cognitive complexity is also affected by peoples' motives; Suedfeld and Rank (1976) showed that revolutionaries thought in very simple terms, until the revolution, whereupon some of them stopped seeing things simply and became cognitively complex. The ones who didn't show this change of thinking generally lost power.

The last word in this section should be left to O'Neal (1971) who showed that when the rater had to choose between the people he was rating, he saw them in more 'black and white', cognitively simple terms, that is, his ratings of their different traits tended to correlate significantly more. It will be recalled that psychologists first became interested in 'logical error' or 'halo' in trait ratings, because they feared it would lessen the value of supervisor's or interviewer's ratings; O'Neal's results imply that the selection interview, where interviewers feel the need to justify their choice, in fact is precisely where the halo effect will be most marked.

## The accuracy of implicit personality theories

Personality research studies the real relationships between items of behaviour, and can discover whether IPTs are correct or not. However, scientific and everyday descriptions of personality and behaviour take different forms; most modern approaches to personality prefer a dimensional approach to a typology. Every individual can be placed on an extroversion dimension; people are not divided into separate classes labelled extrovert and introvert. Most IPTs however, are typological. Indeed, this is one of the basic assumptions of Kelly's personal construct theory. People classify others as good *or* bad, neurotic *or* stable, extrovert *or* introvert. Of course, some thinking about people does use dimensional concepts; people will say that one person is more extroverted than another but not so extroverted as a third. Even so, most thinking about people uses classes rather than dimensions; language itself is very suitable for classifying people and nowhere near so suitable for ranging them on a dimension. IPTs are predominantly typological because there are limits to the number of distinctions people can make in successive comparisons along one dimension. A personality test, like the Eysenck Personality Inventory (EPI), can reliably distinguish seven[1] different levels of extroversion,

[1]   The range of possible scores 0-24 on the EPI suggests twenty-five levels, but error of measurement means that the difference between a score of 14 and 15 is not reliable, whereas the difference between 14 and 19 is.

whereas a human judge probably could not distinguish more than four or five. In fact, Bieri *et al.* (1966) found that people did not even do as well as that, being able to distinguish only from two to four steps. His findings go some way to confirm Kelly's (1955) hypothesis that personality 'constructs' are 'bi-polar', 'strong *or* weak', 'good *or* bad', etc.

Wiggins, Hoffman and Taber (1969) have reported an interesting study on inaccuracy in implicit personality theories of intelligence. Their subjects were presented with case histories of college students, in which a number of items of biographical data were systematically varied; subjects estimated the student's intelligence. Two-thirds of the subjects used vocabulary and school achievement as the main criteria, which were in fact the most accurate cues. A substantial minority used social status and industriousness, which are less accurate criteria; these subjects tended to be authoritarian in outlook. A few subjects used quite irrational criteria; one judge assumed that the sole criterion of high intelligence was emotional *in* stability. Wiggins *et al.*'s results imply that an important part of any training for professional 'person perceivers' like psychiatrists or personnel managers, should be the measurement and, if necessary, correction of their IPTs.

## Sources of error and bias in implicit personality theories

Many IPTs are incorrect; for example, emotional instability is not a good criterion for intelligence. People who rely on incorrect IPTs are not likely to make the right decisions about someone and so are likely to do the wrong thing. Kelly's personal construct theory and the social skill model both emphasize the 'adaptive' role of person perception and argue that IPTs will be changed in the light of experience. However, there is considerable evidence that impressions are often resistent to change. Thus Kelley (1950) told half a class that a speaker would be warm and the other half that he would be cold; the people who had expected him to be cold, saw him as cold, and they participated less in the group discussion. Their impression of him was rigidly held and could not be altered by subsequent evidence. A similar study by Luchins (1957) finds that the first of two conflicting descriptions of a boy called Jim determined the final impression, and the second aspect was ignored. However, he did find that the 'primacy' effect could be abolished by warning the subject against 'first impressions' or by giving them an intervening task. Stanton and

Baker (1942) asked interviewers to get certain items of information from their interviewees and told them the 'correct' answers beforehand; the interviewees actually gave quite different responses, but the interviewers still wrote down the answers they expected to hear. Kahn and Cannell (1957) studied recordings of interviews and found that the interviewers had their ideas about what the subject meant to say, and ignored or interrupted him if he tried to explain what he really meant.

*Evaluative bias*

The bias shown by Kelley's subjects and by Stanton and Baker's interviewers arose because they had been given a 'set' or expectation about what they would see. Luchins's subjects had similarly been biassed by their first information about Jim. If people have expectations about others' behaviour a change in one aspect of their impression may imply changes in others; if someone thinks that 'warm' people are also 'sociable', then changing 'warm' to 'cold' in the description will affect a judgement of 'sociable' also. The prediction is correct; changing one part of a description of a person usually leads to changes in other logically unrelated parts of the impression. However, Asch (1946) suggested that some attributes were more 'central' than others; thus changing these attributes leads to a series of changes, while changing others does not. For example, altering 'warm' to 'cold' affected the overall impression, while altering 'polite' to 'blunt' has little or no effect on the other dimensions. Wishner (1960) subsequently argued that Asch's results were not as puzzling or exciting as they seemed; the 'warm/cold' rating scale happened to be central to the evaluative dimension underlying many other scales, where the 'polite/blunt' scale is not. The more trait scales the altered scale happens to correlate with, the more scales will tend to change when the alteration is made. The central dimension that can shift judgements on all other dimensions is most often an evaluative dimension; if the target is popular, favourable characteristics are attributed to him whereas, if he is unpopular, the rater is reluctant to allow him any good points.

*Motivated bias?*

Wiggins *et al.*'s data on judgements of intelligence and the data of studies like that of Chapman and Chapman (1967) on the use of the Rorschach test, described in Chapter 2, show that people's ideas are often wrong, but even so may be clung to despite clear evidence of their incorrectness. Some of this inefficiency undoubtedly stems from man's limitations as a processor of information; unable to cope with a flood of partly reliable, partly overlapping information, the naïve observer oversimplifies and hence generates an incorrect view of the significance of behaviour.

However, one of Wiggins *et al.*'s findings points to another possibility; subjects who wrongly thought hard work and social class were indicators of intelligence in students, tended to have an authoritarian personality. The authoritarian, according to Brown (1965), owes his respect for authority and the upper classes and his distrust of intellectuals to the way he is brought up; his views about correlates of intelligence are not just superficial opinions, easily changed by contrary information, but are, in a sense, part of his personality. Authoritarianism could also explain the results of another well-known study. Gollin (1954) made a film of a girl showing her behaving both promiscuously and kindly. A lot of people who saw the film found the two facets of her personality inconsistent, that is, counter to their IPTs. Gollin classified their reactions to the inconsistency. Half ignored one of the characteristics and described the girl as kind or promiscuous, but not both. The rest admitted both characteristics, some trying to explain how they were related and some not. Given that sexual repression and rigidly conventional outlook are characteristic of authoritarians, one could confidently predict that those of Gollin's subjects who thought a girl could not be both kind and promiscuous would have higher authoritarianism scores.

*Projection*

The idea that inner conflict can disturb the way someone sees other people is not new; Freud listed, among his defence mechanisms, the 'projection' of repressed tendencies onto other people. A latent homosexual vigorously – too vigorously – denies his own impulses, but gives himself away by accusing others of homosexuality. What he is afraid to see in himself, he sees in other people. The experimental evidence is inconclusive because of the problems of obtaining criterion data, on whether someone 'really' is a latent homosexual or 'really' is mean, and because it is difficult to show that ratings of self and others are distorted by sexual conflicts, rather than by more mundane forces. A well-known study by Sears (1936) appeared to show that students who were rated by their fellows as 'mean' tended to rate their fellows as mean (meanness is an 'anal' character trait, according to Freud, derived from toilet training experiences, and therefore conceivably an occasion for repression and projection). Unfortunately this interesting result does not stand up to close scrutiny; Wells and Goldstein (1964) repeated Sears's study exactly and found that college students just did not call their peers mean often enough to locate a 'mean' group for study. Only if meanness were perversely defined as a score greater than 3.3 on a scale 1 'generous' to 7 'very stingy', could Sears's results be replicated. However, Wells and Goldstein, like Sears before them, also found that above averagely generous people also 'projected' generosity, which makes little or no sense as a Freudian mechanism, and seems rather more likely to be an artefact of the way the subjects used the seven-point scale.

Murstein and Pryer (1959), in a useful review of the concept, distinguished another, non-Freudian type of 'projection'. 'Rationalized projection' is not a defence mechanism, is not motivated solely by sexual repression, and does not depend on particular stages in the individual's 'psychosexual' development.

Relatively little attention has been paid lately to motivated distortions of person perception. A welcome exception is a recent study by Cantor (1976) which showed how people's usual ways of seeing others are related to their own motives. Experts were able to predict from the person's Repertory Grid the dominant motives that emerged from their Thematic Apperception Test protocols. A college male, whose major construct on the Grid was 'member of the liberal upper class, interesting and intelligent, insulated by wealth' against 'politically reactionary "redneck" ' was correctly judged to have TAT needs of dominance, aggression, autonomy and exhibitionism. Two general principles emerged from the study by which it is possible – up to a point – to predict how someone will 'construe' others. Rule 1 says that if a person places a strong positive value on some characteristic in other people, he or she is likely to have a need corresponding to (or similar to) that characteristic. Rule 2 says that people appraise others in terms of whether those others will be receptive to them and will fulfil their needs.

## Four origins of implicit personality theories

A consideration of why IPTs are often inaccurate leads to a review of sources of bias and systematic error. Consideration of how people come to distort the way they see others leads to a further question – where do people get their theories about other people from? Sarbin *et al.* (1960) distinguished four main sources of IPTs: induction, construction, analogy and authority. Their discussion is largely speculative, for there is little satisfactory research on this question.

'Induction' means experience. If someone has consistently observed that people who are intelligent do well at school, then he has formed this IPT by induction. Providing his observations were accurate, and based on an adequate sample, his theory will be correct.

The same does not apply to rules acquired by 'construction', that is, those that the person invents for himself. Some are highly personal, but many others are public property; for example, it is commonly believed that men who keep their money in purses are mean, or that people whose eyebrows meet in the middle are murderers. Such ideas usually have no foundation in reality, nor even in the person's experience: they have been 'constructed'. Sarbin *et al.* do not explain why people should invent false ideas about others, but it is likely that many ideas are defence mechanisms: for example, the man who thinks women untrustworthy may be rationalizing his unsuccessful relations with women. Seeing the enemy, in wartime, as unprincipled, degenerate, perverted, etc., justifies all the unprincipled attacks made on them. To the extent that 'constructed' ideas about others do satisfy needs in the judge, they will be highly resistant to change.

Sarbin *et al.* also include, as 'constructions', deductions from theories, including scientific theories. If a theory allows the deduction that racially prejudiced people are less stable than the norm, the idea is said to be constructed. It might be better to distinguish between irrational constructions, that will generally be wrong, and deductions from theories, that will be correct, if the premises are correct; it would certainly be more flattering to scientific psychology to distinguish its theories from irrational inventions.

The third source of ideas about others is 'analogy'. The person reasons that because someone reacts in a particular way, everyone else or everyone in a similar class of people will do the same. The man who is success with a short, blonde girl at a party meets another short, blonde girl a week later and expects to get on as well with her – but unfortunately for him, his conversational gambits remind her of someone she took a violent dislike to; both reasoned by analogy. Models for analogy include the family, friends, teachers and, most important of all, oneself. There is a strong tendency to assume others think and behave like oneself, and in the absence of better information this is a sensible strategy. Analogy with other people is basically the same as induction, only based on a narrower sample. Research on 'identification' in children shows the child adopts the parents' beliefs and attitudes including possibly the parents' reactions to other people.

The fourth source of ideas about others is 'authority'. The person is told that 'people who are rich are also lazy' and accepts it. Most ideas about what is wrong or unacceptable behaviour come from parents, school friends, workmates, possibly in that order of importance. Much research has been done on the moral development of children, showing at what age they first acquire ideas about right and wrong and how they apply them. Much work has also been done on group norms, that is, shared beliefs about correct behaviour, opinions and attitudes, in family, social work and groups (see Krech, Crutchfield and Ballachey, 1962, for a review). People also get more general ideas about personality, behaviour, moods, etc., from others, in the shape of gossip, and from books, cinema and television.

Sarbin et al. give a good account of where the detail of IPTs comes from, which is not the same as explaining why they exist in the first place. Reverting to the theme of Chapter 1, people have a strong need to categorize and make sense of the endless flow of behaviour. Not content with covering a whole complex area of someone's behaviour with a blanket term like 'maladjusted', the perceiver goes on to oversimplify the oversimplification by covering 'maladjusted' in turn with an even larger blanket, which on close inspection turns out to have the label 'people I don't like'.

The evidence that IPTs are oversimplifications is already quite impressive, but the final testimony will be left to D'Andrade (1970, cited by Schneider, 1973) whose work reflects that of Bartlett (1932). Bartlett showed that an originally complicated and rather peculiar story was simplified over time to fit the teller's own ideas; D'Andrade found that the same was true for impressions of people. Ratings made immediately after meeting someone are 'cognitively complex' and 'idiosyncratic', giving perhaps a true reflection of the other's behaviour; as the meeting receded into the past, the ratings came to resemble the usual 'dictionary' structure, centred on evaluation, as the perceiver twisted and turned them into the usual way of seeing things.

# INFORMATION USED IN PERSON PERCEPTION

## Past, present and future issues

It is less easy in this area to identify lines of research no longer pursued, than to point to ones that don't seem worth pursuing any further. Interest in the cruder types of research on facial expression of emotion has diminished somewhat but is not entirely dead. The more pointless type of research on stereotypes, by contrast, flourishes unabated; numerous studies are published every year showing that people can draw inferences about others on the basis of a single piece of information such as eye colour or hair colour or the possession of a non-WASP[1] surname. Similarly mindless studies on the inferences that are, or can be, drawn from non-verbal behaviour are beginning to accumulate, but otherwise research on non-verbal behaviour is more promising, both in its subtlety of approach, exemplified by Kendon's work, and in the development of useful conceptual frameworks by Argyle and Ekman. Unfortunately the same cannot be said of attribution theory, where crude and clumsy experiments abound, and no attempt seems to have been made to make an initially vague theory more precise; in fact the opposite seems to be happening, with attribution theory jargon being used more and more generally to account for everything, and hence for nothing.

Within attribution theory the theme that could most usefully be developed is the attribution of responsibility, where a combination of sensible externally valid paradigms and close attention to developing a theory complex enough to account for the data should yield results. Otherwise the two most obvious gaps in the account of the way information is used in person perception are the issues of how outlook, attitudes and personality affect perception, and how people acquire their ideas about others.

---

[1] White Anglo-Saxon Protestant.

# PART III
# ACCURACY IN
# PERCEIVING OTHER
# PEOPLE

The next three chapters are concerned with aspects of the accuracy with which people sum each other up. This has been touched on already, in Chapter 2, when the view that intuitive perceptions of other people are also infallible was mentioned, and has been mentioned here and there, when discussing research on clinical prediction and implicit personality theories; the time has come to look at the issue in greater detail.

The study of how accurately people see each other has theoretical relevance, practical relevance in everyday encounters and relevance for applied psychology. Personal construct theory and Argyle's account of the social skill model emphasize, as do other broader theories like the phenomenological approach of Snygg and Combs (1949), that people respond to what *they see*, not to what *others see*, nor to what is '*really*' *there*; if their perceptions of what is there are incorrect, or at least not shared by others, their behaviour will be less appropriate. The theoretical relevance of research on accuracy is closely linked to the everyday relevance; people are constantly forming impressions of others' moods, intentions and dispositions, and acting on those impressions. The accuracy of these impressions is a topic worth studying on its own, as are the related issues of what sort of person makes what sort of accurate perceptions about what sort of other person. The practical everyday relevance of accuracy research shades gradually, through such fields as marriage guidance counselling and social work, into the areas of principal relevance in applied psychology – psychiatric diagnosis, and the selection of employees, students and the like.

It is necessary to emphasize the importance of accuracy research, because its value has been questioned by people, who, one supposes, have not experienced for themselves the effects of making wrong predictions about other people. What does motivate at least some people to question the feasibility or value of accuracy research is the fact that it is methodologically more difficult than it first appears.

# PROCESSES OF PERSON PERCEPTION

## Past, present and future issues

The argument that perceiving other people depends on a faculty of intuition is now more of historical interest than current concern. The work of Sarbin *et al*. has established definitely that perceiving other people depends on some sort of mechanism, which can be uncovered by research. The question of what the mechanism might be still remains open. Sarbin *et al*.'s account in terms of categorical inference does seem to represent the way people actually think, even though, as Meehl points out, it is logically suspect. Since then two main approaches to the mechanisms underlying person perception have emerged. The first, and more fully developed, follows the line Meehl suggested, and found that a model based on correlation and regression does give the best answers; however the work of the Oregon Research Institute clearly shows that the lay perceiver cannot think in these terms. Perhaps the most important task for researchers in the future will be the further exploration of the way the layman uses multiple conflicting cues, in a more realistic experimental paradigm than the Asch-Anderson one. The second development from Sarbin *et al*., the social skill model of Argyle and Kendon, extends the inference model to cover perception during actual encounters, and is notable princi-pally for giving further impetus to the extensive body of research in non-verbal behaviour, some of which is reviewed in the next chapter.

There are so many pitfalls, some so well-hidden, that the first of the three chapters – Chapter 7, 'Cronbach's Components' – is devoted entirely to them. The second chapter – Chapter 8, 'The Good Judge' – reviews some of the research on everyday perceptions people make of each other, concentrating particularly on perception with engaged and married couples, and including a discussion of whether there is 'a good judge of others' and what characteristics define him (or her). The last chapter – Chapter 9, 'The Interview' – concentrates on personnel selection and psychiatric diagnosis, by interview; other ways of selection in diagnosing people are mentioned, but a comprehensive review of tests, questionnaires, observations and rating systems is beyond our scope.

# 7 'CRONBACH'S COMPONENTS'

## The methodological problems of accuracy research

> Does your husband like his steaks:  rare
>                                      medium
>                                      well-done
> From the BBC TV quiz programme *Mr and Mrs*

'Tests' of this sort feature in radio and TV quiz programmes, and often appear in newspapers and womens' magazines. The subjects in many experiments on 'accuracy of person perception' are set much the same task. They look simple, straightforward, valid tests of 'accuracy' but they are not; they are a 'Pandora's Box of statistical and methodological artefacts' (Cronbach, 1955). Explaining why will make this chapter heavier going than the others.

The question of how accurately one person can assess another's character attracted attention early in the history of scientific psychology. Numerous studies on the correctness of 'subjective estimates' of intelligence followed the introduction of the intelligence test, e.g. Hollingworth (1916), while, at the same time, the vast literature on the identification of facial expressions of emotion began to accumulate (reviewed by Woodworth, 1938). The modern – or recent – period of accuracy research began shortly before the Second World War (Estes, 1938) and flourished in the ten years after it. This work, mostly using ratings and multiple choice formats, was checked by the publication of a series of critiques by Cronbach and others.

Since then research has proceeded haltingly, except for a steady stream of papers on the accuracy of clinical judgement.

Research on the accuracy of person perception may be discussed under five headings. There will be some people to make the perceptions, and some people to be perceived, and there will be a limited body of information about the latter for the former to use – 'Judges, targets and information'. The people making the judgements will do so in a format prescribed by the experimenter; the various 'forms of judgement', the next heading, each have advantages and disadvantages. The experimenter requires a 'criterion' against which to mark his judges' perceptions right or wrong; finding a good criterion is very difficult. Finally, the experimenter has to find a system of 'scoring' that won't introduce artefacts, and in particular needs to be able to cope with the problems of 'stereotype accuracy' and 'assumed similarity' which often allow his subjects to get the answer right, but not in the way the experimenter meant him to.

## Judges, targets and information

An experimental test of accuracy of judgement requires some people to do the judging – judges – and some people to be judged – targets. The information on which the judges base their opinions may be extensive and more-or-less uncontrolled, as when a group of friends judge each other (e.g. Taft, 1956) or when a school teacher judges his pupils (Magson, 1926, and many others) or the information may be tightly controlled, highly specific, infinitely replicable – and somewhat artificial – like photographs, handwriting, drawings, MMPI profiles, Rorschach protocols. A good compromise between control and richness is the tape-recorded interview (Weiss, 1963) or the filmed interview, used extensively by Cline (1964) and Crow (1957). Cline's films of five-minute stress interviews have been used in a number of subsequent studies, e.g. Conklin and Ogston (1970), and are the nearest to a standard test of person perception yet devised.

The information given to the judges should be relevant as well as controlled, although it's difficult to say what is or is not relevant, given the current state of personality research. Blanchard (1966) devised a simple operational test of the relevance of information, namely the extent to which it is correlated with the items to be judged, and demonstrated that judges could predict quite accurately from relevant information, but no better than chance from irrelevant information. The experimenter next decides what inferences his judges should be asked to make; emotional states and personality traits seem to be the favourite choice. A wise experimenter ensures that the judges aren't either required to make wild guesses from completely unhelpful information, or left simply to cast their minds back to remember something they have already been told word for word. A wise experimenter also ensures the judges will find the task meaningful: Clements (1967) chose his twenty-four 'problem behaviours' for unhappily married couples only after discussions with a number of such couples. Interestingly enough, he reports that his happily married group found many of the items in his test irrelevant.

The 'programmed case' method has been used by Dailey (1963) and Fancher (1967); the judges predict, on the analogy of programmed learning, a chronological series of events from one person's life and are given the correct answer after each judgement, so that they can learn about the target person as they go along, as they might in a real encounter. This method, like Cline's films, offers a useful compromise between experimental control, and approximation to real perceptions of others.

## Forms of judgement

The experimenter next decides in what form the judge is to make his judgements; he can choose from six or more possibilities.

### FREE DESCRIPTION

Everday judgements of other people are generally in free description form, as are many formal and professional judgements. Free descriptions are inconvenient to the experimenter, because they are difficult to score, and because they are unlikely to be comparable across judges. Fancher (1967) found the ability to produce recognizable descriptions of people was unrelated – indeed slightly inversely related – to the ability to predict specific behaviour, which casts doubt on the generalizability of much research to everyday life.

### MATCHING

The judge is given one, two or more sets of information from one set of subjects, and asked either to match the information to the subjects, or the sets of information to each other (Vernon, 1936). In a typical experiment, Taft's (1956) judges matched a series of mosaic designs to the people who produced them. The matching method featured frequently in studies of the validity of projective tests, such as the Rorschach.

RANKING

The judge places subjects in order of a characteristic such as intelligence. This method was used extensively in early research, e.g. Hollingworth (1916), but was later supplanted by ratings and multiple choice methods. More recently Berlew and Williams (1964) have used the conceptually similar paired comparisons method. Ranking differs from rating, because it requires relative judgements, rather than absolute ones, and because it cannot take account of unequal differences.

RATING

The judge is asked to 'guess the amount of a trait' the person has, as McHenry (1971) put it. He assigns a number on an arbitrary scale to each target, to indicate the level of intelligence, extroversion, etc. he considers that person to possess. Sometimes judges rate traits based on personality theories or inventories, such as Murray's needs (Estes, 1938) or the MMPI (Crow and Hammond, 1957). Alternatively judges rate interpersonal relationship and feelings; for example, Suchman (1956) asked people to predict ratings of self-confidence, etc. following a group discussion. Steiner and Dodge's (1957) judges rated a curious mixture of traits, including interest in classical music, religiosity and behaviour consistency.

Studies on rating personality proliferated in the early part of the century (see Eysenck (1970) for a good review of the research). Most of this research looked at tests and ratings 'upside down', using the ratings to validate other personality tests, rather than the tests as the criterion for the correctness of the ratings. Occasionally judges are asked to estimate on a percentage scale – essentially a 100 point rating. This may be justified, despite the 'magical number seven plus two'[1] on the grounds that judges are accustomed to thinking in percentages. Sometimes – as in the American college grade system – the raters have

---

[1] It has long been known that people cannot reliably use more than nine scale points.

to make their ratings conform to a normal distribution. While convenient for the statistician, the forced normal distribution method undermines one of the rating method's main advantages – that ratings can be made immediately after each sample is seen, and don't require the judge, as do ranking, matching and sorting, to see all the targets before making any judgement, or else to alter earlier judgements in the light of later ones.

MULTIPLE CHOICE

Ranking and rating methods force the judge to think in terms of dimensions; multiple choice does not. Typically, the judge predicts which of a number of responses the target made. For example, Dailey (1963) and Fancher (1967) constructed biographies of people, structured so that the judge's task was to say which of several possible responses the person actually made on a specific occasion. Cline's 'Behaviour Postdiction Test' is similar, except that the judge says what the person's *habitual* response to a particular situation is. The multiple choice method is a good representation of one of the ways people think about other people – they often do wonder 'what someone is going to do next'. Almost all research has imposed the researchers' categories on the judge, with the possible exception of the studies of psychiatric diagnosis.

By far the commonest task is to predict what answer the target gave to an item on a personality inventory. McHenry (1971) refers to this as the 'guess what he would write' method. Most of the popular inventories have been used in this type of experiment at one time or another, even the vocabulary test of the Wechsler-Bellevue intelligence test (Crow and Hammond, 1957). The use of inventories introduces a serious confusion – is the judge supposed to predict what the subject *really* does, or what he says he does? As people frequently do not tell the truth when completing inventories the distinction is important. The problems of using questionnaires are discussed further in the sections on choice of criterion and stereotype accuracy.

SORTING

The judge places the target people in a number of categories. Thus Toch, Rabin and Wilkin's (1962) judges sorted out thirty-six photographs into twelve of Jews, twelve of Protestants and twelve of Catholics. Studies of clinical judgement often require judges to sort MMPI profiles into neurotic and psychotic. Providing the categories are familiar to the judge, the sorting method has all the advantages of the multiple choice method, and the added virtue of avoiding some artefacts.

Some studies use the Q-sort technique, in which the judge sorts items rather than subjects. In a typical study (Borke and Fiske, 1957) judges sorted a set of 100 statements into categories, approximating a normal distribution, according to whether they were more or less descriptive of the subject, and then did the same for 100 postcards of paintings, according to whether the subject liked them. The Q-sort is popular in studies of clinical judgement, e.g. Silverman (1959).

NOMINATION

The judge names the most extroverted and least extroverted person he knows; it thus resembles conceptually the ranking method. This method is not much use for studying accuracy of person perception, except at a very crude level, but is used widely to validate inventories (Eysenck, 1962).

**The Criterion**

An experiment on the accuracy of judgements won't get far without some way of identifying what will count as 'the right answer'. The size and intractability of the criterion problem varies according to the judgement being studied.

OBJECTIVE CRITERIA

The criterion for judgements of social class (Tudor, 1971) although not perfectly reliable and objective, is solid by the standards of psychological research. Research on prediction of specific behaviour also has a fairly good criterion – what the person actually does or did. Research on things like response to treatment, length of hospital stay, as well as that on prediction of future delinquency (Mannheim and Wilkins, 1955) also has a more-or-less objective criterion. Some recent studies (e.g. Schroeder, 1972) have used a film of a subject being offered a series of choices – e.g. to extract a spike from a piece of wood or hammer it further in, to break a lightbulb or water a pot plant. The film is stopped just as the subject is about to announce his choice and the judge tries to predict what it will be.

'What the person actually did' is usually reported, not observed, so the reports may be fallible. Trankell (1972) staged a dispute in a class and tape-recorded a complicated sequence of events, culminating in an apparent shooting. Reports immediately after the event were not reliable; witnesses got the sequence of events wrong, estimated the time intervals very inaccurately, couldn't remember who said what, and in what order, and so on. Trankell's criterion was his tape-recording, so that he was in effect studying the validity of the type of report Cline and others have taken as a criterion.

Even when behaviour is accurately recorded or reported, it may nevertheless be inherently unreliable. Schroeder (1972) does not report the re-test reliability of subject's choices in the choice test, but it is certain that not all twenty choices would be the same if the procedure were repeated after an interval. If the test item covers 'characteristic' responses or 'usual' behaviour, not what happened on a particular day, unreliability should be less of a problem – or one wouldn't talk of 'characteristic response'. However, 'characteristic' poses the question 'how characteristic'? Chapter 1 discussed the problem, raised by Mischel (1968), that behaviour isn't as consistent as personality theorists, psychologists, and people in general tend to think. Cline (1964) met this objection by obtaining reports from the target, and from his family, fellow students, etc. and by using only items where all agreed the behaviour was characteristic. He also chose the incorrect alternatives 'so as to eliminate even partial occasional kinds of behaviour'. McHenry (1971) comments 'With respect to Cline, this is difficult to believe'. The central difficulty of personality research has been that behaviour just isn't that consistent.

Many studies have used personality inventories both as judging instruments and as criteria. The criterion appears water-tight – namely what he actually did write – but there is a serious ambiguity in this method – is judge predicting what subject does or what he says he does?

CRITERIA FOR EMOTIONAL EXPRESSIONS

The difficulties encountered so far can be dealt with by experimental ingenuity and refinement, but efforts to find criteria for emotional expressions and personality traits run into logical and philosophical difficulties. Early research on emotional expression, reviewed by Woodworth (1938), relied on various forms of 'face' validity – the intention of the person making the expression, or the opinion of the experimenter. When the expressions were shown to a group of judges and those not readily recognized eliminated, a further criterion was added – a group consensus. Some experimenters sought more objective criteria, and also wanted more realistic expressions. Landis (1929) exposed his subjects to a series of events calculated to evoke different expressions – a nasty smell for disgust, a pistol shot for surprise or electric shock for pain, etc. Sherman (1927) adapted this approach to infants, using, for example, a pinprick for pain. Munn (1940) went one step further on the road to realism and obtained press pictures of people facing execution, winning a fortune, etc. The criterion in these studies was 'evoking stimulus'; the expressions evoked varied considerably, but not according to what had evoked them, so the method proved unsatisfactory. Krause (1961) discussed the problems of identifying emotional states, given that different ways of doing it gives different results, and concluded that no one criterion is sufficient and that a combination of what the person says he's feeling, with some measure of physical changes in his face or body, is better.

CRITERIA FOR PERSONALITY TRAITS

The greatest difficulties arise for the experimenter who wishes to find a criterion for personality, so that he can say, at least for the purposes of his experiment, that person A is 'really' more extrovert than person B. There are essentially four possible criteria in trait rating and trait ranking experiments – group consensus, expert opinion, self-rating and ranking and test data.

*Group consensus*
This is simply the average rating or ranking given to the target person by a number of others who know him; Sears's (1936) well-known study on projection used the average rating of the target by his friends as the criterion for his 'meanness'. Inasmuch as meanness is a socially defined trait, the opinion of a number of people who know the target well ought to constitute a satisfactory criterion. Yet one may question whether the target's meanness is consistently displayed to all the class, and in fact whether the ratings of those who'd experienced the meanness deserved to be submerged in the average of those who hadn't. One may also question whether an investigation of distortions in the way people perceive meanness – caused by their own inner conflicts –

should use perceptions of meanness as its criterion of 'real' meanness. Even if the whole class did point to one of their number as mean, this might merely indicate that he was unpopular, and seen as having an undesirable trait. In fact the problem with Sears's study and its several replications was that no one was identified as 'really' – seven out of seven on the ratings – mean and that the 'mean' group were defined somewhat unsatisfactorily as those below the group average for generosity.

*Expert opinion*

Some studies take 'expert opinion' as a criterion; Estes (1938) used the consensus opinion of Murray's personality assessment team. This criterion still finds favour in clinical work. Graham (1971) used Meehl's assessment team's opinion as the criterion for diagnostic status, and Sines (1959) used the therapist's Q-sort for the patients, after ten hours therapy, as criterion for judgements from test material. This choice of criterion obviously poses the question – how does one know the expert is right? There is plenty of evidence, e.g. Oskamp (1962), showing that experts have little or no superiority in judgement.

*Self-rating and ranking*

This resembles group consensus or expert opinion, in that it still compares one person's judgement with another's, but differs in that it acknowledges the fact. Dymond's (1949) well-known 'empathy test' used self-rating as criterion. Her judges predicted the target's self-rating on five-point scales of friendliness, self-confidence and leadership, and the instructions made it clear that the judges' task was to predict the target's self-rating, and not to assess his actual leadership. Steiner and Dodge (1957) demonstrated that predictions of a person's self-ratings, and assessments on the same scale of 'the person as he really is' differed so much 'that it seems unreasonable to regard the two techniques as interchangeable'. Many subjects find rating scales difficult to use, so the task of predicting, in terms of the scale, how someone else uses it is likely to be even more difficult; there is evidence to suggest people resolve the difficulty by using response sets (see 'Social desirability'). The self-rating criterion continues to find favour, especially in research on marriage, e.g. Murstein and Beck (1972), where it is more reasonable to expect one partner to be able to predict the other's self-rating of happiness, marital harmony, etc.

*Test data*

The final criterion is less 'circular' than the others but hasn't been used much to study the perception of traits. (Many studies use personality inventories but most analyse the data item by item.) Several early studies, e.g. Hollingworth (1916), used intelligence tests as criterion, and Crow and Hammond (1957) used the MMPI as criterion for ratings of the target 'as he really is'. Intelligence tests are reliable and objective, which makes them excellent criteria. Personality tests are not quite such good criteria, being less reliable and less objective in that the person describes his own behaviour, so his report has more the status of a self-rating.

One could plausibly argue that it is pointless to look for a good criterion for judgements of personality traits, because there can never be a way of measuring them that does not depend on someone's judgement. Traits are socially defined, and exist in the eye of the beholder. The experimenter can check whether someone's assessment of a particular trait in a particular person accords with the generally accepted view, but no more. Inventories and other tests are merely elaborate, devious and imperfect ways of recording the same type of information. For many traits this argument is undeniably correct. It would be absurd to suppose there could ever be a way of defining or 'measuring' politeness that did not ultimately depend on one person's opinion of another's behaviour, but it depends on one's view of personality whether one applies this principle to all traits. If everyone thought a particular individual unintelligent, it would be nevertheless possible to prove them wrong with intelligence test data. Could the same be done for any personality dimension? Not at present, but if theories like that of Eysenck (1967) about the biological basis of personality are correct, it might one day be possible to measure extroversion or anxiety-proneness objectively and reliably.

## Scoring

For most judgement tasks, the scoring system follows naturally from the structure of the task, but difficulties arise in the scoring of rating data. Early research by Magson (1926), Rugg (1921) and others correlated ratings and criterion test data. Estes (1938) devised the index of squared differences $\sqrt{\Sigma D^2}$ – where D is the absolute difference between criterion and predicted ratings. This method, in various forms, was used in most subsequent rating research, until its deficiencies were noted by Cronbach (1955).

Cronbach pointed out that difference scores are unsatisfactory measures of accuracy of perception. It will be useful to consider a concrete example. Table 7.1 presents ratings, by three judges of ten targets on 'narrow-mindedness', together with criterion scores. The first judge has a raw difference score of 20 which makes him the 'worst' judge. In fact all his ratings are 2 points lower than the criterion; if this constant error were eliminated, he would be completely accurate. Cronbach calls such constant errors differences in 'level'. Their significance is uncertain. The judge may be actually underestimating the narrow-mindedness of the ten subjects; on the other hand, the constant error may be a 'leniency effect' – a tendency to rate people favourably. It may mean no more than the judge is uncertain how to use the numerical scale; he may intend 3 to mean the same as the criterion rater meant by 5.

*Table* 7.1  Imaginary data, representing the ratings by three judges of ten subjects, on a single trait

| Subjects | A | B | C | D | E | F | G | H | I | J | |
|---|---|---|---|---|---|---|---|---|---|---|---|
| Criterion Rating | 5 | 6 | 5 | 4 | 5 | 7 | 4 | 5 | 4 | 5 | |
| Judge 1 | 3 | 4 | 3 | 2 | 3 | 5 | 2 | 3 | 2 | 3 | difference score - 20 |
| Judge 2 | 5 | 8 | 5 | 2 | 5 | 9 | 2 | 5 | 2 | 5 | difference score - 10 |
| Judge 3 | 5 | 5 | 5 | 5 | 5 | 5 | 5 | 5 | 5 | 5 | difference score - 6 |

The second judge scores 10, which makes him second best of the three. He has correctly identified the mean score as 5, and has correctly perceived that subjects 1, 3, 5, 8 and 10 score at the mean. He has also correctly perceived the direction of the deviations from the means of the other subjects. His only error lies in his estimation of the size of the deviations, for he over-estimates them all by 2 or 3 scale points. Cronbach calls this an error of 'spread'. Once again the meaning of the second judge's ratings is uncertain. It could represent a real difference in his opinion or just a different way of using the rating scale.

The third scores only 6 which makes him 'the best judge'. He has achieved his high accuracy in a very odd way, by giving everyone the same score. The other two judges had correctly perceived which subjects deviated from the mean, and in which direction, but judge 3 hasn't done either. Cronbach calls this an error in 'correlation'.

There is obviously something wrong with a scoring system that favours judge 3 over judges 1 and 2. In fact when difference scores are used, any judge who correctly estimates the average score of the subjects is automatically at an advantage, and there are several reasons, including 'social desirability' and 'assumed similarity', why people often do find it easy to guess the average response. Cronbach and others regard the components as genuine and important aspects of the judgement process. Smith (1966) arranges his book in terms of Cronbach's components, suggesting that they should be studied in their own right. Certainly Cronbach's observations are very valuable when considering judgement tasks that usually employ numerical ratings, such as school and university examinations, clinical ratings or supervisors' ratings in industry, but the researcher on accuracy does not have to use ratings, if they present problems.

The difficulties Cronbach describes had been observed previously. Vernon (1953) noted 'The outstanding defect of this type of scale is the variations in standards and distributions adopted by different raters.' This defect can be remedied by using standard scores, or by correlation. Cronbach (1955) suggested a scoring system based on deviations from overall means – essentially standard score analyses. Cline and Richards (1960) devised the Interpersonal Accuracy (IA) score, with two components, one of which (IAr) is calculated by correlating the judge's ratings and criterion ratings for each trait. Christensen (1970) devised a 'refined difference score', in which ratings of each target are expressed deviations from that judge's rating of the norm for that type of person, e.g. 'typical male white college student'. Criterion ratings are expressed in the same way and differences squared and summed. Other authors, from Valentine (1929) through Exline (1957) to Gabennesch and Hunt (1971), have simply correlated the two sets of ratings without further ado. The obvious next step – to require the judges to rank subjects, not rate them – was taken by Cook and Smith (1974). Ranking of course ignores differences of 'level' and 'spread', but then the whole point of Cronbach's analysis is that 'level' and 'spread' are as likely to reflect response biasses as judgements of real differences in what is being rated.

Cronbach's message has not reached all quarters of the psychological world and studies using ratings and difference scores still appear. Laing, Phillipson and Lee (1966) appear to be using some form of difference score, although the account of their method of analysis is so obscure it is difficult to tell. Two studies using ratings, in a repertory grid format (Ryle and Lunghi, 1971; Watson, 1970), also appear to have used difference scores, although again it is difficult to be sure, since the data were analysed by a computer program. Some research on marriage, e.g. Murstein and Beck (1972), still uses rating and difference score methods.

## Stereotype accuracy

Research aims to develop measures of 'differential accuracy', the prediction of what a *particular* person will do in a particular situation, but often fails to distinguish differential accuracy from stereotype accuracy – the prediction of what *most* people will do in a particular situation. In rating studies the person who correctly perceives or happens to arrive at the average rating is automatically at an advantage. Similarly, in multiple choice judgements, if the person can predict that one response is more likely than the others he can use this insight to advantage. For example if the Eysenck Personality Questionnaire (EPQ) were used in an accuracy experiment[2] it would probably be found that judges could predict targets' responses with much better than chance accuracy. This would reflect the fact that the EPQ contains twenty 'psychoticism' items, which few normal people check. Scarcely any normal person replies 'no' to the question 'was your mother a good woman' – which tends to make the judge's task easier. In fact it changes it completely; instead of making judgements about people he is making judgements about inventory items. Since most inventories contain many items that are answered the same way by most people, the problem is a major one. It's also an old one, in a different guise; Remmers (1950) reviewed a number of pre-war studies on 'faking' inventories, which showed that people could predict the average or desirable response to a variety of inventories.

The problem is not confined to questionnaires. Wherever the responses to be predicted are not equally probable, people may be able to use the fact to achieve stereotype accuracy. It is of course unlikely that the responses will be equally probable, i.e. that of twenty-five subjects exactly five will make each of five responses, unless the experimenter takes steps to ensure it. It is the failure to take account of 'stereotype accuracy' that renders most 'Do you really know your

---

[2] Which, to the best of the author's knowledge, it hasn't been.

spouse' type quizzes worthless, but many research studies have the same failing. Schroeder (1972) and Tomlinson (1967) make no reference to controlling for stereotype accuracy although the judgement tasks used – the filmed binary choice procedure (see p.106), the Gough Adjective Check List – almost certainly require it.

There are several reasons why responses usually won't be equally probable. The first is simple real similarity – the fact that people do have things in common and often tend to make the same response in the same situation. The use of homogeneous samples, like college students, naturally increases similarity. Other sources of stereotype accuracy arise from the judgement task used; inventories and ratings are particularly prone to introduce stereotype accuracy.

### STEREOTYPE ACCURACY AND QUESTIONNAIRES

Studies using inventories introduce stereotype problems, because of 'response sets' in the way people answer them (see Vernon (1964) for a good review). For example, the California F scale, measuring authoritarian personality tendencies, has an 'acquiescence bias'. The more often the person says 'yes', the more authoritarian he scores; some people tend to say 'yes' regardless of the question. More pervasive is the 'social desirability set' – the tendency to present oneself in as favourable a light as possible, and in person perception research to view, or to appear to view, others in a favourable light too. These response sets could possibly allow people to judge accurately more-or-less unawares. People don't necessarily make a conscious decision about the likely usual response; if judge and target both opt for the 'socially desirable' answers, the judge achieves accuracy, not because his reasoning is correct but because his response bias matches that of the target.

### STEREOTYPE ACCURACY AND RATINGS

Similar problems beset rating experiments. As Cohen (1953) noted in a critique of Nottcut and Silva's (1951) rating experiment, ratings usually have a normal distribution, centred at the mid-point of the scale – or to put it another way, most people use the mid-point of the scales, and not the extremes. If the judge realizes this – or unthinkingly follows the same habit himself – his ratings will be more 'accurate'. Sometimes ratings are skewed by the operation of the social desirability set. Lindgren and Robinson (1953), in a critique of

Dymond's work, noted that most people describe themselves as 'fairly friendly' – point four on a five-point scale – perhaps because being 'fairly friendly' is a social norm for most people. If the judges follow a related norm, that one should not describe others as unfriendly, their scores will match the target's ratings, without any real judgement being involved.

## PREVENTING OR CONTROLLING FOR STEREOTYPE ACCURACY

There are several ways of dealing with the stereotype accuracy problems. Some experimenters require their judges to make predictions with little or no information about the target. Weiss (1963) used this technique to eliminate items that could be predicted without any information about the target. Sometimes judges make predictions for stereotype targets – the average patient (Silverman, 1959) or the average college student (Gage, 1952). Gage's frequently cited study demonstrated that estimates of the 'average college student's' Kuder Preference Schedule were a better fit for individual targets than predictions judges made specifically about those targets, after they'd watched their expressive behaviour. If a well-standardised inventory is being used, the experimenter can discard those items evoking a markedly skewed response. An unpublished study by McHenry using the Maudsley Personality Inventory, found that eliminating all such items also largely eliminated any possibility of the judge predicting with better than chance accuracy.

The most elaborate attempt to control for response sets was made by Hatch (1962), who devised a 'Forced Choice Differential Test' that eliminates all artefacts, needing 20 hours of computer time to do it. The judges – who were managers – predicted *which of two* statements about supervisor – subordinate relations – *both of two* subordinates *disagreed* with. By careful choice of items Hatch tried to eliminate all statistical and assumed similarity artefacts. For example, some items are more controversial and so more likely to provoke disagreement, and if the judge can identify these – an instance of stereotype accuracy – he can achieve a good score, without making any judgement about the individuals. This was prevented by equating both items for controversy.

Researchers on marriage and friendship, e.g. Schiller (1932), developed the 'random pair comparison' as a simple control for similarity artefacts. When it is used in accuracy research, the judges' predictions are compared with criterion data for randomly selected targets, as well as with the true targets, and only if the latter are predicted more accurately than the former, is the judge credited with differential accuracy of perception.

It isn't always possible or desirable to make the alternatives to be predicted equally probably. Many important behaviours that the layman or expert is called on to predict have what Meehl and Rosen (1955) call a 'low base rate' – they don't happen very often. Most murderers don't do it again and can be safely released, but a minority are dangerous. Most psychiatric patients don't kill themselves, but a proportion will. The expert's problem is that people aren't impressed by all the non-events he successfully predicts, but focus their attention on the released murderer who kills again, or the patient who manages suicide. It would obviously be silly to construct a test of the expert's ability to predict rare events which made the alternatives – further violent crime/good behaviour, suicide/survival – equally likely, just as it would be silly for the expert to maximize his score by employing a stereotype and saying no one will re-offend, or no one will kill himself. In fact, rare events are very difficult to predict; research on the clinical prediction of suicide (Murphy, 1972) is largely a story of failure; nor has research on the prediction of crime and delinquency (Mannheim and Wilkins, 1955) had more than limited success.

Stereotype accuracy can also be avoided by changing the task, so as to prevent judges attributing the same response to most targets. Sechrest and Jackson (1961) regarded their raw data on predictions of leisure interests as essentially data about stereotype accuracy and, in a second stage of their study, required their judges to sort eight targets into four categories – which two targets play football, which two read books, etc. – to yield a measure of differential accuracy. The matching method also avoids the stereotype problem, because it prevents the judges attributing the same response to most or all targets.

## Assumed similarity

One particular response bias has exercised researchers more than any other – the tendency to assume that others will respond like oneself. Scodel and Mussen (1953) showed that people assumed that others shared their own authoritarian personality or, as Hastorf and Bender (1952) put it, 'projected' their authoritarian tendencies onto others. Highly authoritarian judges made accurate assessments of authoritarianism for highly authoritarian targets, but couldn't do the same for liberal targets, a finding which could be more parsimoniously described by saying that highly authoritarian people assume everyone else is highly authoritarian too. Rabinowitz (1956) confirmed Scodel's findings by asking people high and low in authoritarianism, to estimate the average student's responses to the scale. Highly authoritarian people thought the average score was 125, which compared with their own mean score of 116, and the actual average of Rabinowitz's sample of 83. The tendency to 'project' authoritarianism is not general however. Schodel's liberal-minded judges tended to assume others scored in the middle range – which no one actually did in Scodel's studies, because his subjects were chosen as either authoritarian or liberal. A substantial body of research on friendship and marriage (reviewed by Berscheid and Walster, 1969) has shown that friends and couples, while having more in common than random pairs, almost always exaggerate their similarity.

Hastorf and Bender (1952) pointed out that real similarity, assumed similarity and accuracy were mathematically linked; given any two, the third could be calculated. They suggested that accuracy scores should be 'corrected' for real similarity, so that the judge would only get credit for saying correctly the other person wasn't like him. Blanchard's (1966) subjects predicted the responses of 'typical' members of different occupations to the Strong Vocational Interest Blank, using ten items where the target's responses was the same as the judges and ten items where it was different.

The assumed similarity effect makes it difficult to study the relations between similarity and accuracy of judgement, and between friendship and perception of friendship. When judges correctly predict that others will do the same as them, is it accuracy or 'warranted assumed similarity'? When people correctly perceive that others like them, is it accuracy, or is it the logical outcome of the fact that people (a) reciprocate liking, (b) assume others reciprocate liking (Taguiri, 1958)? In fact people don't always assume similarity – Scodel's low authoritarians didn't – and don't assume *complete* similarity. Several studies have reported correlations between real similarity, and 'accuracy' of perception; the larger the correlation, the more powerful the operation of assumed similarity bias. Correlations are generally positive, but low; for example, Corsini (1956) reported five correlations ranging from 0.22 to 0.53, the latter figure alone being statistically significant.

Baker and Sarbin (1956) take issue with Hastorf's comments on assumed similarity, and with his 'correction' for it. They point out that 'assumed similarity' is just one of many principles used to make inferences about others. Singling out judgements based on this principle and disallowing them is an irrational procedure – they ask 'why not "correct for" ethnocentrism, conceptual rigidity or any other variable that might possibly mediate achievement?'

## Conclusions

The impression may have been created by now, that the whole business of trying to measure the accuracy of person perception is so hopelessly complicated that it should be abandoned. This was the impression created on many researchers by Cronbach's critiques; the apparent difficulty of doing research led many workers in the field, by a familiar process of rationalization, to argue that the issue wasn't important, wasn't worth studying experimentally, or even that it didn't exist. This conclusion is quite obviously false. People do have to make decisions about what other people are like or what they will do next. Their decisions are often wrong, even when those taking them are supposed to be experts at the job. Ways of finding out if someone is any good at summing up others and predicting their behaviour are needed; the refinements in experimental technique since Cronbach's critiques have provided them. The would-be investigator of psychiatric diagnosis, selection interviewing, social work assessment, or marriage and friendship merely has to take simple steps to avoid obvious and less obvious methodological traps.

# 8 THE GOOD JUDGE OF OTHERS
## Accuracy in everyday encounters

> He wished, as often in the past, that he was a really mature man who 'knew' things like that 'by instinct'. He tried to draw a mental picture of someone who looked like Emilia and who 'was just waiting for you to try it on so she could slap your face', and then of someone who looked like Emilia and who 'was bloody sitting up and begging for it'. Both pictures were highly plausible and resembled each other even more closely than they resembled Emilia.
>
> (From Kingsley Amis's *I like it here*)

Some people are confident they understand others, and can predict their next move, or sum up their character; others are not so confident. The one group is as likely to get it right as the other, for the certainty of a person's opinions about other people is essentially unrelated to their correctness.

The social skill model – see Chapter 2 – divides perception of others into two – initial impression, and feedback that may modify the first impression – and holds the perception of how the other person is, coupled with one's knowledge of how one wants him or her to be, determines one's actions. An incorrect first assessment will lead to the wrong move being made, and incorrect interpretation of the effects of a first move will make things worse, which all tends to imply that most people, profiting from the speedy recognition of their mistakes, will become accurate judges of character and intention. Somehow they mostly fail to do so; the most striking finding to emerge from the extensive, jumbled literature on 'accuracy of person perception' is how very inaccurate most people are most of the time.

PERCEIVING BEHAVIOUR AND PERSONALITY

Archer and Akert (1977) have devised a Social Interpretations task, in which short sequences of filmed encounter are followed by simple, relevant questions which have definite answers – such as which man won the tennis match? or, which of the women is the mother of the child? Pure guesswork would give an average score of 6 out of 16, which compares with an average of 8.85 right for subjects who saw the films, and a dismal 5.50 for subjects who merely read the script. Schroeder (1972), using a similar procedure, got similar results – 9.4 correct predictions from 17 binary choices, an excess over guesswork of just one right answer. The critic could say that the tasks used in these studies are trivial or unrepresentative – although Archer and Akert's Social Interpretations look eminently reasonable – but much the same conclusions emerge from other studies. Fancher's (1969) judges 'post-dicted' key choices a person made at important moments in his life, e.g. (to paraphrase and condense somewhat) 'In the Second World War was he a war correspondent in London, or did he do a master's degree in political science, or did he join the US Marines and serve in the Pacific?' Twelve 'post-dictions', each with three possible answers, implies a guesswork score of 4; judges actually achieved a score of 5 to $5\frac{1}{2}$. In Fancher's experiment, as in other 'programmed case' studies, the judges are told what the target actually did on each occasion, before making their next 'post-diction', so that, in theory, they learn something about him, or at least don't get too far down the wrong track; in practice, the information doesn't seem to lift their overall accuracy much above chance level.

If people perform poorly on the 'guess what he will do/did do next' task, what of other common techniques? Many studies provide data on the 'guess what he would write' task, where judges predict the way targets complete a inventory. Dymond (1954) found her two groups, with scores of 33 and 38 out of 55, not very far above chance level of 27 or 28 – although doing perhaps a little better than Schroeder's judges. Gabennesch and Hunt (1971) examined the ability of students to predict how other students had completed the California F scale, measuring authoritarian outlook or 'implicit fascist tendency', after a discussion of 'radio, television and the movies', and found that the predicted total score and actual total scores correlated an average (median) 0.47 and 0.24 in two groups of judges.

Accounts of rating studies – the 'guess the amount of the trait' method – rarely include any estimate of the accuracy of the judges, and commonly employ such dubious criteria – 'expert opinion' or 'group consensus' – as to make such an estimate meaningless. An exception is an early study by Magson (1926) on ratings of pupils' intelligence by tutors and fellow students; on average these ratings agreed with group tests to the extent of a correlation of 0.53, which is quite impressive bearing in mind the upper limit of 0.87 set on the possible value of this correlation by the reliability of the tests. Magson cites several earlier studies showing that estimates of intelligence were moderately well correlated with test data. More recently Cook and Smith (1974), using a rank order procedure, found that ranking of students for extroversion agreed with test data on average 0.48 but for neuroticism only 0.07.

## PERCEIVING LIKING AND SOCIAL INFLUENCE

Some work has been reported on the perception of liking and disliking. Tagiuri (1958) reports that people can say who in a group likes them, with a better than chance accuracy, but admits that the assumed liking problem makes this finding hard to interpret. He also reports that people are much less accurate at guessing who dislikes them and suggests various explanations for this, for example, that people show dislike less plainly than liking. However, the more parsimonious explanation might be that it is an 'assumed liking' effect; if people always assume that those they like return their liking, they will inevitably be bad at seeing dislike. Tagiuri also reports that people are good at judging who likes who in the group, as opposed to who likes them; there is no reason to expect an 'assumed liking' effect if the perceiver isn't involved in the comparison. Crow and Hammond (1957) report above chance accuracy on a variety of sociometric tasks involving judgements of leadership, co-operation and likeability. More recently Stein, Geis and Damarin (1973) found that the leadership structure of groups could be predicted, with varying degrees of accuracy, by people who watched films of the discussions, and in a later study Stein (1975) found that the subject could do this equally well from reading a script of the discussion or from watching a silent film; the information is evidently conveyed both verbally and non-verbally.

PERCEIVING MOODS AND EMOTIONS

Early studies on moods and emotions underestimated people's ability to identify the emotions portrayed, partly because they counted a response as wrong unless the perceiver used the precise word the experimenter had in mind. If the perceiver said 'contempt' when the experimenter intended the photograph to portray 'disgust', the answer was considered to be wrong. Woodworth (1938) re-analysed previous data and found that the various emotions can be grouped into six categories so that errors in identification are rarely more than one step away from the correct answer. His six categories are: love, happiness/mirth, surprise, fear/suffering, anger/determination, disgust/contempt. Schlosberg (1954) showed that if the ends of the scale are joined up to form a circle, Woodworth's findings about the distance of errors still holds. Further work by Schlosberg and others finds that two or possibly three dimensions – pleasantness/unpleasantness, attention/rejection and (possibly) level of activation – can be used to describe facial expressions.

A few studies have reported that some emotions are more easily identifiable than others. For example, studies using the 'Feleky' pictures find that fear, horror and surprise were more easily identified than other emotions, but one doesn't know whether this is a general trend, or specific to the expressions produced by the actress Feleky (1914) photographed. Thompson and Meltzer (1964) studied the way a number of subjects expressed various emotions and found that happiness, love, fear and determination are identified more accurately than disgust, contempt and suffering; they suggest, however, that their subjects may have been identifying embarrassment rather than love. Davitz (1964), studying vocal expression of emotion, found that subjectively similar emotions, for example, joy and cheerfulness, are more difficult to discriminate than dissimilar emotions; this finding is implied by Woodworth's six category system.

The 'pin a label on the photograph' method has many obvious disadvantages; a recent study by Buck (1976) tries to avoid some of them by using short films of students' natural facial expressions evoked by 'sexual, scenic, unpleasant or unusual' slides. Various samples of judges could say what sort of slide the target was looking at about 50 percent of the time (against 20 percent chance level). Buck, Miller and Caul (1974) also demonstrated that the ability of students to express their reaction to various slides through their facial expressions was inversely related to their psychophysiological reaction to the slides, which seems to give some support to 'hydraulic' models of emotions – what isn't expressed outwards will make itself felt inside.

In most studies the expression is presented without any context. Langfeld (1918) found that suggestions made to judges by the experimenter were readily accepted by them, showing that it is possible to read into the photographs a variety of meanings. Frijda (1958) showed that giving the photographs a context affects judgements of them considerably, and went on to suggest that the expression alone gives only very basic information about the person's mood – for example, that he is displeased, and that knowledge of the context is required to distinguish between the finer shades, such as disgust and anger.

The shortcomings of this body of research have been mentioned in Chapter 4 – the face, like the voice, gesture and posture, conveys other messages besides crude emotions like rage or joy, and conveys them in a subtler way, needing subtler research methods than those commonly employed.

## FROM COURTSHIP TO MARRIED BLISS

Too much person perception research has studied opinions formed by people, who have no pressing need to form them, about people they have little contact with, and will never meet again outside the laboratory. A courting couple are in a much better position to get to know each other, besides having much stronger reasons for needing to. A number of studies of how clearly couples see each other have appeared over the last twenty years, and have yielded mixed results. Even before boy meets girl, both partners have serious misconceptions about the others' wants and intentions. Hewitt (1958) found that 69 percent of men wanted girlfriends who were 'ambitious and industrious', but only 48 percent of women thought men valued these qualities, and that 80 percent of men thought women regarded the men's physical appearance as crucial, when only 21 percent of women actually thought this. Balswick and Anderson (1968) asked a number of college students what they expected should happen on a first date, and what they thought the other person would expect to happen. This was to see whether the boy's and girl's ideas of what to do coincide, or whether they misunderstand each other and go out on their date with inconsistent ideas about how to behave. College men were asked if they expected a girl to let them kiss her after a first date, and college women if they expected a man to want to; slightly more than half said yes to these questions. Next the subjects were asked to predict what the other sex thought was expected, to see if the girls think the boys expect a kiss, and if the boys think the girls expect them to try. The results showed conclusively that the two sexes systematically misunderstood each other.

These misunderstandings take an interesting form that has highly significant consequences. Whereas only half the men and women actually expected or wanted to kiss after a first date, rather nearer three-quarters thought it expected of them. This inaccuracy of students' perceptions of what the opposite sex thinks will tend to cause an increase in permissiveness, for if everyone thinks the people around them are more permissive or sexually active than they really are, and if they live up to this wrong impression, it will be made true – an example of self-fulfilling prophecy. In fact, another study by Jackson and Potkay (1973) found that college women generally overestimated rather than underestimated the proportions of their peers who were not virgins; on average they thought less than half of other college women were virgins, whereas in fact more than half – 57 percent to be exact – were. This misperception is also likely to give rise to a self-fulfilling prophecy.

Kirpatrick and Hobart (1954) found that the ability of couples to predict each other's answers to a Family Opinion Survey was higher if they were married, as opposed to engaged, and higher in engaged couples than in couples merely dating. This finding might be dismissed as a 'glimpse of the blindingly obvious', if it were not for two facts; firstly, the tendency Kirkpatrick and Hobart found was very modest, and secondly, subsequent research has not always been able to find even modest correlations between length of relationship and accuracy of perception. Udry (1963) found that most of the variance in couples' predictions of each others' 16PF[1] inventories was accounted for by random error, with a tendency to assume similarity, and accurate prediction, each accounting for around 10-15 percent. Murstein (1972) found a modest but reliable tendency for inaccurate perception of each other on the Marital Expectation Test to predict 'poor courtship progress'; Udry (1967), employing the possibly less relevant 16PF, was unable to relate the outcome of a liaison – breakup/mar-

---

[1]   16 personality factors.

riage – to accuracy of perception.

Attempts to prove that happy marriages are characterized by the partners seeing each other's point of view clearly – a very plausible and widely held assumption – have not generally been successful either. Corsini (1956), using Q sorts, and Clements (1967), using rank orders of marital grievances, found no differences between stable, happy marriages and unstable, unhappy ones. Dymond (1954) found a very modest advantage – 38 against 33 out of 55 predictions – for happy couples, while Murstein and Beck's (1972) best correlation, out of 48, between adjustment and accuracy of perception, was only 0.37.

Udry (1963) points to one of the reasons for this initially puzzling finding – assumed similarity; married couples seem to get by much of the time in ignorance of what the other really thinks, comfortably assuming the other shares their views. Byrne and Blaylock (1963) found very limited similarity of opinion – on Rokeach's Dogmatism Scale – but much greater perceived similarity, correlations of 0.69 and 0.89 against 0.30 and 0.44. Some schools of thought use words like 'pseudo-mutuality' to describe families whose members allow their differences to go unrecognized behind a public front of agreement and solidarity; using such disparaging terms implies it's a bad practice. If it is a bad habit, it's a very common one. Steiner (1955) questions the assumption that a person who sees clearly what other people think about him is always benefitted by his insight, and points out that it would often merely undermine self-confidence and paralyse social interaction. Sociologists like Goffman (1956) point out that much of the time people are putting on different fronts, for different occasions; seeing through someone's front or 'self-presentation' to what they're really like, or at least to what they're like on other occasions, sometimes causes acute embarrassment, rather than leading, as the social skill model or personal construct theory predicts, to a smoother or more satisfying interaction.

THE GOOD JUDGE – FACT OR IDEAL?

Mischel (1968) has re-emphasized the point that people – including psychologists – tend to assume that for every word there must be a concrete reality, even though the evidence for the existence of many personality traits – as patterns of behaviour consistent over a number of different occasions – is poor. Is there such a person as 'a good judge of others', or is he as big a myth as the 'good leader'?

Vernon (1933) found very few correlations between a large number of tests, although there was slight evidence of correlations within four groups of tests: accuracy of predicting ratings of self by others, accuracy of ratings of others, accuracy of perception of strangers (which includes recognition of emotion tasks), and a set of tests involving writing character sketches; Vernon found no evidence for generality of ability across tasks and little evidence of generality within tasks. Wedeck (1947) found that various tests of identifying emotions and personality from photographs correlated together, but didn't correlate with a test of ability to detect lies. Taft (1956) found a small correlation between ability to estimate group responses to the MMPI and a task involving rating traits like 'persuasiveness'. The latter uses a global difference score, pooled across all traits and all target persons, so is possibly a measure of stereotype accuracy, which would account for its correlation with the group test. Neither test correlated with a test of matching mosaics to their authors, which required judges to make decisions about particular individuals, rather than about people in general.

Two other large-scale studies produce conflicting results. Crow and Hammond (1957) gave their subjects fifteen tests, divided into three groups. In the first group the subjects saw films of the targets and judged them on a 'reticence test', on a vocabulary test and on a global trait rating test. The second group was a series of sociometric tests of leadership, co-operation and liking, and the third was a group opinion test. None of the tests correlated together. Only six of a possible 105 correlations were significant, and these were all small. Even tests that might be expected to correlate, such as the various sociometric tests, did not. On the other hand Cline and Richards (1960) did find high correlations between various tests – Behaviour Postdiction Test, sentence completion, opinion prediction, adjective check list and trait rating – that his subjects took after seeing films of the targets. Cline and Richards analysed the trait ratings into stereotype and differential accuracy and found that each correlated with the other tests, although the correlations with stereotype accuracy were generally higher. They suggested that some people were accurate overall because they distinguished accurately between different targets (differential accuracy), others because they estimated the average score (stereotype accuracy), and some because they did both. Bronfenbrenner, Harding and Gallway (1958) reached similar conclusions. Cline and Richards suggested that accuracy of judgement is a general trait but, like intelligence, has 'group factors'; certain groups of tests correlate together more highly than others, but all tests correlate positively. This interesting theory has not been followed up, nor has any research correlated any of these perception tasks with 'social intelligence' tests.

## CHARACTERISTICS OF GOOD JUDGES OF OTHERS

The notion of an all-purpose good judge of others – good at every task and on every occasion – has proved oversimplified, but it is still possible to seek correlates of good judgement on a more limited scale.

### Sex

'Intuition' is popularly supposed to be a prerogative of women but the hard evidence on sex differences in person perception is rather inconclusive. Taft (1955) reports that, of nine studies of emotion recognition, three found a slight superiority for women, one a slight superiority for men and five found no difference between the sexes. The literature could be more accurately summarized by saying that sex differences, when they occur, usually favour women, but that they do not usually occur. Hoffman (1977), reviewing later studies, agreed that there was no evidence that women were better at recognizing emotions, but did find a reliable trend, in six out of sixteen comparisons, for women to react emotionally to other peoples' emotions. The greater 'empathy' (see Chapter 2) of women was observed in grown women, girls and newborn infants, which led Hoffman to wonder if biological sex differences, as well as culturally determined ones, might not play a part. More generally, studies reviewed by Maccoby and Jacklin (1975) found no sex differences in other person perception tasks.

### Age

Various early studies, reviewed by Taft (1955), indicate that children get better at identifying facial and vocal expressions of emotion as they grow older; several more recent studies have shown the same, again concentrating on recognizing emotional states. Solomon and Ali (1972) compared content and tone of voice cues, and found children relied more on content. Borke (1971) found that even three-year-old children could say what another child's reaction would be to losing a toy or eating a favourite snack, contrary to the widely held Piagetian hypothesis that children are 'egocentric' – unable to see another's point of view. Dymond, Hughes and Raabe (1952) showed that children improve markedly between the ages of seven and eleven in their ability to report correctly which of their classmates liked them; otherwise little research has been reported.

*Intelligence*
Taft (1956) confirmed the results of earlier studies, finding a low positive correlation between intelligence and tasks of rating traits like 'social assertiveness' or deciding which person had produced which mosaic design; in fact a correlation of 0.37 with 'best performance' (from five intelligence tests) is quite impressive, bearing in mind that the judges were all graduate students, representing a very restricted range of ability. Sechrest and Jackson (1961) on the other hand, also using student subjects, found no correlation at all between intelligence and either stereotype or differential accuracy measures in a behaviour prediction task. Wolfe (1974) used adolescents as subjects, to predict how two teachers would complete Cattell's 16PF questionnaire, and found that their ability to do so correlated with their intelligence and with their 'conceptual level' – a measure of the abstractness of responses to a task involving completing paragraphs. On balance there does seem to be a link between intelligence and ability to perceive other people accurately, but more research is needed to give a fuller account of it.

*Personality*
Various early studies, reviewed by Taft (1955), found that unstable people are poorer at trait rating tasks and are not, as sometimes is suggested, more sensitive to others as a consequence of being more sensitive to themselves. Particularly interesting is a finding that accident-prone workers have less empathic ability. Scodel's work (Scodel and Mussen, 1953) found ample evidence that highly authoritarian people assumed others were as authoritarian as them, but didn't show that authoritarians were poorer judges of others, as their supposed possession of rigid closed minds would seem to imply. However, Gabennesch and Hunt (1971) did find that authoritarians were worse at perceiving the rank order of authoritarianism within their groups than were people with a more liberal outlook.

Two studies, Dymond (1950) and Taft (1956), reported that good judges were more sociable, although Taft also suggested that detachment in social relations is characteristic of accurate judges. Grossman, cited by Cline (1964), found differential accuracy related to tough-mindedness and a tendency to be empirical and nonconforming. Sechrest and Jackson (1961) found no correlation between differential accuracy and a variety of measures: MMPI scales, sociometric ratings, repertory grid and Rorschach scores, etc. They did find correlations between stereotype accuracy and sociometric ratings of pleasantness and predictability, and absence of psychopathic deviance on the MMPI. Chance and Meaders (1960) found that judges with good differential accuracy show a pattern of self-ratings of independence, strong-mindedness, participation in social relations and absence of introspection.

Bronfenbrenner et al. (1958) found that sex of judge and sex of subject is related to personality characteristics of good judges, which could account for the inconclusive results of other research that didn't consider sex differences. The pattern illustrated in Table 8.1 was found.

Table 8.1  Personality characteristics of good judges.

|  | of male subjects | of female subjects |
|---|---|---|
| Male judges | resourceful | tactful |
|  | dominant | tolerant |
|  | outgoing | timid |
|  | not very tactful |  |
| Female judges | submissive | submissive |
|  | reasonable | insecure |
|  | accepting | inhibited |
|  |  | unattractive |

If the personality of good male judges is examined without considering the sex of the subject, the contrasting descriptions cancel each other out and no correlations are found. The results are reasonably similar to these of Chance and Meaders, who used only male subjects and judges and found good judges are high on affiliation and dominance but not very reflective. Grossman also studied only males and his results are reasonably similar. Bronfenbrenner et al. also considered stereotype accuracy and concluded that the good judge of stereotypes tends himself to fit American middle-class ideal stereotypes; the men were seen as outgoing, self-assured, uninhibited and rather objectionable, while the women were controlled, well-socialized and competent. The latter result is similar to Sechrest and

Jackson's findings.

The results of these studies are interesting. Bronfenbrenner *et al.*'s data suggest that other studies fail to find any significant relationship because they do not take account of sex differences. There is also an encouraging similarity between the Bronfenbrenner findings about male judges of male subjects, and Chance and Meaders' data, and between Sechrest and Jackson and Bronfenbrenner *et al.* about women judges with stereotype accuracy, even though different tasks and different personality measures are used. However, the picture of the good male judge that emerges is rather unexpected. The good male judge of males is described as a rather insensitive, aggressive person while the good male judge of females is described as very ineffectual. The good female judges are described slightly more favourably. The results suggest that Steiner (1955) is right and that the good judge of others might not be socially polished and confident. Bronfenbrenner *et al.* point out that they were dealing with the first impressions; a different picture might emerge in an established relationship.

Berlew and Williams (1964) took another approach to getting a clearer picture of who is a good judge, and were able to show that people with a 'high need for achievement' were poorer at predicting others' self-perceptions of achievement-oriented traits like 'keeness', when the task was 'made achievement relevant' by being presented as a test of intelligence; the authors explain their result by saying in effect that the performance of ambitious subjects, given a supposedly testing task, was disrupted by the anxiety it caused.

*Mental illness and character disorders*

Research on all aspects of person perception in psychiatric patients has been sparse and unsystematic, with the sole exception of studies of schizophrenic personal construct systems. Of schizophrenics, it is known that they are poor at emotion recognition tasks (Davitz, 1964), at predicting word associations (Milgram, 1960), and at synchronizing their speech with that of the person they are conversing with (Matarazzo and Saslow, 1961). More generally it has been observed in numerous studies (Argyle, 1969) that their social behaviour is grossly abnormal; they do not orient towards others, do not look at them, and do not produce appropriate replies to anything said to them. On the other hand, the work of Braginsky and Braginsky (1967) implies that many schizophrenics can converse normally, and even make a good job of deceiving others, if they feel like it. Helfand (1956) showed that partly recovered schizophrenics were just as good as control subjects at predicting someone's Q sort. However, chronic schizophrenic patients were not; the distribution of their accuracy scores centred exactly on chance level. Research findings so far leave it uncertain whether schizophrenics' social perceptions are poor through lack of ability, or lack of interest in the task, and whether the lack of interest is caused by 'institutionalization' or something else.

Paranoid schizophrenics by definition perceive things and people around them incorrectly. Their misperceptions take many and bizarre forms. Weston and Whitlock (1971) describe a case of a rare and striking delusion called the 'Capgras Syndrome' in which the patient is convinced that his nearest and dearest are not themselves any more, but that their place has been taken by imposters disguised as them. Colby (1977) reviews several theories of paranoia, and dismisses among others the Freudian theory of repressed homosexuality: 'I love him – I mustn't love him – I hate him – he hates me'. He prefers a type of 'perceptual defence' theory, according to which the paranoid person is afraid of being found wanting, and watches everything and everyone for anything that might reflect this, whereupon it is immediately attributed to someone else.

Gough and Petersen (1952) constructed a test for detecting psychopathic patients, based on the assumption that they do not perceive other people's feelings and do not predict their behaviour accurately; Gough (1948) reports that, as a consequence of the psychopath's inability to understand other people's reactions, he does not understand punishment and disapproval.

Although some of the symptoms of neurosis – touchiness, over-sensitivity, insensitivity – imply that neurotics' perceptions of others will frequently be incorrect, little or no research has been reported.

TRAINING AND EXPERIENCE

Davitz (1964) shows that the accuracy of identification of emotions by face and voice can be improved by giving the judges the 'correct' answers during a practice session; Jecker, Maccoby and Breitrose (1965) similarly find that 'knowledge of results' or 'feedback' improved teachers' perception of pupils' comprehension. Feedback also improves predictions made from the MMPI (Graham, 1971) and from programmed cases.

Several studies (e.g. Oskamp, 1962; Silverman, 1959) found that clinical experience confers little or no superiority in predictive accuracy, nor does training as a student counsellor (Altmann and Shymko, 1970). A number of studies, starting with Estes (1938), and reviewed by Weiss (1963), found that psychologists were actually worse than average at summing up other people. Fancher (1966) found a social science outlook a liability in 'postdicting' important choices a person made, and found rather than accurate judges used, on the Repertory Grid and in studying his life-histories, 'objective' cues, like sex, age, occupation and religious affiliation. Perhaps training as a psychologist encourages people to use 'intervening variables' like 'extroverted' or 'dominant', which aren't as helpful as the inference from one specific detail to another. In fact Campbell and Dunnette (1968) found that the only measurable effect of 'sensitivity training' – intended to make people see each others dispositions and feelings more clearly – was to increase the amount of psychological jargon they used; no increase in genuine accuracy of perception was recorded.

## Conclusions

Ability to sum up others is not a general trait, so there is no class of person who can always 'read other people's minds' and always know what they are going to do next. Anyone vain enough to suppose that he is a member of this special class is probably deluding himself by not bothering to check the correctness of his predictions, by casting horoscopes so broad and vague as to be confirmed by any outcome, and by making his prophecies fulfil themselves by his own behaviour. The larger class of more modest people who envy 'the good judge of others' are possibly prompted by a realization of their failures, to assume that because they are bad judges of others, there must be good judges and that their good judgement will be exercised at all times.

It is curious, given that almost everything that could usefully be factor-analysed and much that couldn't, *has* been factor-analysed, that no one has yet applied this technique to accuracy of person perception, to yield an account of the abilities and sub-abilities involved. Such an account would be of great value of further research on the characteristics of people who, without training, happen to be accurate judges and on ways of improving the performance of people who are not.

# 9 THE INTERVIEW
## Accuracy in professional encounters

Now think carefully before you answer this. If you were fat as well as stupid, would you be as proud of being fat as you are of being stupid?

From *That Uncertain Feeling*
by Kingsley Amis

Amis finishes his ideal interview for getting the right man to work in a public library with this curious question; anyone who has had many interviews will know that fiction is only slightly stranger than fact, and will probably have been asked questions almost as rude, silly or irrelevant. The reasons people have for giving interviews are many and various, ranging from determining someone's genuine need for social security, through assessing his suitability for employment, to describing his fundamental personality dynamics. On all these occasions the interviewer is trying to reach a conclusion about someone, inferring from what he says and does in the interview to what he is like or what he will do in the future. The interviewer is doing much the same as the man trying to decide what his wife's reactions to something will be, or the subject in a person perception experiment trying to say how someone else completed a personality questionnaire.

The greater part of the research effort has been directed at selection interviewing and psychiatric diagnosis, but many of its conclusions apply equally well to areas like child guidance, survey interviewing, student counselling, social work, vocational guidance, and even to the broader fields of education, law and commerce.

## The selection interview

### HISTORICAL BACKGROUND

A 1957 survey of US firms found that 99 percent used interviews to select their staff; no doubt a figure of that order could be obtained in Britain or any other industrial country of the West. Interviews are also used to select people for training and education, but not on such a large scale; British universities for example don't usually interview would-be students.

Selection by supposed merit has a fairly short history (and one wonders if, given the trends in social policy such as anti-discrimination laws, it mightn't have an even shorter future). In a primitive community selection isn't needed, because there aren't that many people to select from or jobs to select for; in a farming village everyone farms. Town life brings a range of jobs, some nicer and better paid than others; town life also brings nepotism, patronage and a class system, which often prevent the best man for the job getting it.

Formal selection procedures – interview and examination – were, according to Northcote Parkinson (1958), borrowed from Imperial China and first used in the West in the British Civil Service in 1855. In the twentieth century sheer weight of numbers, the millions of soldiers conscripted in both World Wars, demolished the old systems of selection and promotion that depended on personal acquaintance and social background. The US Army employed from 1917 the 'Army Alpha', the first mass intelligence test; the British did the same from 1943. The American Army intelligence and personality tests of the First World War were released for civilian use, and they and many other tests seem to have been more widely used in the US then than tests are in Britain even now. The Second World War saw further developments in selection methods. In Britain the three services devised elaborate methods of selection for both specialized trades like radio mechanics and for officer selection. The War Office Selection Board (WOSB) was set up, providing a lengthy and elaborate assessment routine for officer candidates, and making efforts to test its own validity (Vernon and Parry, 1949). The post-war history of selection and the interview is less dramatic. The WOSB method found favour also with the British Civil Service, becoming the Civil Service Selection Board (CISSB). Numerous selection systems of unknown validity are in use on both sides of the Atlantic, while research on validity has made most people (in the minority who read such reports) cautious, if not actually despairing. In the USA especially, the issues of 'fair employment' and minority groups are presently forcing selectors to look at their methods again.

## SELECTION METHODS

The personnel manager who wishes to hire the best four applicants from the twenty who answered his advertisement has essentially five ways of doing it:

(a)  References, testimonials, or peer ratings, which are descriptions of the candidate by people who know him well.

(b)  Personality tests, which, as Cronbach (1970) points out, are like a statesman's diary – an account of how their authors would like others to see them.

(c)  Tests of ability, including general intelligence tests, are hard to fake, but not always reliable or valid, nor always feasible.

(d)  Background information. Adopting Mischel's (1968) dictum that past behaviour is the best predictor of future behaviour would make life difficult for people with criminal records or histories of frequent illness, absenteeism or non-achievement.

(e)  The interview which, with the reference, is the favourite method.

Shortage of time, restrictions on who can use them, union pressures, and general suspicion combine to make personality and intelligence tests rare in British selection systems. Cronbach (1970) and Anastasi (1976) give an account of their use in North America.

Interviews vary widely. Sometimes there is one interviewer, sometimes three, five, or even fifteen. Sometimes the three or more interviewers see the candidate separately, sometimes he is reduced to speechless terror by their assembled mass. Some interviewers are psychologists or psychiatrists, some personnel managers, some general management, or local worthies. Sometimes the interviewer is friendly and tries to establish rapport, sometimes he tries stress methods, and quite often he has no particular strategy. Sometimes he has a clear idea of what is wanted – a 'job description' – and a checklist of things to ask about, and a rating system for converting his impressions into a decision.

The sort of interview common enough in British universities, where an assembly of a dozen or so people, with no experience or training in selection and no idea what they're looking for, ask whatever questions come into their heads, and reach a decision by lengthy undirected wrangling, is obviously a waste of time; to re-apply a comment from Northcote Parkinson, 'its results are all about us and are obviously deplorable'. The question is whether a good interviewer, asking sensible questions, listening to the answers, and attaching the right weight to each of them, can out-perform any of the other methods, or can add anything to them, or can even do better than a man equipped with a pin, a blindfold, and a list of the applicants.

RELIABILITY AND VALIDITY OF THE SELECTION INTERVIEW

Research on interviewing has been reviewed several times, by Mayfield (1964), Ulrich and Trumbo (1965) and Wright (1969). Interviewers usually agree with each other, to the extent of inter-interviewer reliability coefficients ranging from 0.62 to 0.90, which Ulrich and Trumbo describe as 'lower than usually accepted for devices used for individual prediction'. Webster (1964) showed that interviewers tended to develop a shared stereotype of 'the good applicant' (but not of the bad applicant), which would account for their ability to agree with each other.

But are they agreeing about the right candidate? Is 'the good applicant' actually a good applicant? Determining the validity of interviews, as of any other selection method, is a slow, expensive and uncertain enterprise. In its ideal form it has probably only ever been done once, for ideally one should validate a selection method by testing all applicants, *employing all applicants*, measuring success, and then correlating success with tests and combinations of tests, to pick out the most discriminating measures. The only organization with the resources to do this so far has been the US Air Force, who took an unselected entry into flying school in the Second World War. Most of the reasons why unselected entries aren't used more often need no comment, but blind faith that selection procedures must have some use, and fear of what might be learned from unselected entry to medical school or the higher ranks of the civil service, are less obvious possible reasons.

Nearly all studies settle for the less radical method of correlating selection tests with success within the minority of selected applicants. This 'restricts the range' of quality of applicants because, unless the selection tests are completely useless, they will weed out some of the obviously bad applicants. 'Restricted range' necessarily restricts the size of the correlation, so many studies quote 'adjusted' validity coefficients corrected for attenuation. For example Landy (1976), reporting a study on the use of interviews to select Florida policemen, found that interview assessments of motivation correlated 0.25 with 'technical competence' on the job before correction, and 0.33 after. This was the second highest correlation Landy found (the highest being 0.34) and these results are typical of the validity coefficients usually reported. Ulrich and Trumbo's review found that validities of less than 0.50 were the rule and validities of less than 0.30 very common. Elaborate procedures employing intelligence tests, exams, biographical data and interviews do not fare much better. A recent follow-up study of British Admiralty Interview Boards by Gardner and Williams (1973) got similar results to earlier validity studies on WOSBs (Vernon and Parry, 1949) and CISSBs (Vernon, 1950), in that the best single validity coefficient was 0.40. Similar findings emerge from several detailed studies of ways of selecting Peace Corps volunteers in the USA; Harris (1972) found that a one-hour interview by a psychologist showed 'an essential lack of predictive validity', while a 'board rating' – the consensus of between seven and twenty-four experts – generated 'predictions with a high degree of consistency, even if not always with a high degree of accuracy'.

A selection technique with a validity coefficient as 'good' as 0.50, which would be exceptional, still makes a lot of mistakes. If half the candidates were to be accepted, Table 9.1 shows that 17 bad candidates would join 33 good ones, while the other 17 acceptable candidates would be missed. If only one in five are to be taken on – a much more likely proportion for the better sort of job – a validity coefficient of 0.50 means that bad candidates accepted outnumber the good (Table 9.2), and should the validity be a more modest 0.25, then selection gives such a slight superiority over the man with the pin and the blindfold – six good candidates accepted against four – as not to justify the time and money it costs (Table 9.3).

THE CRITERION PROBLEM

The selection interview is an exercise in accuracy of person percep-

*Table* 9.1  Percentage of good and bad candidates accepted and rejected, where the selection procedure has a validity of 0.50 and half the candidates are accepted.

|  | good | bad |
|---|---|---|
| accepted | 33 | 17 |
| rejected | 17 | 33 |

*Table* 9.2  Percentage of good and bad candidates accepted and rejected, where the selection procedure has a validity of 0.50 and one-fifth of the candidates are accepted.

|  | good | bad |
|---|---|---|
| accepted | 9 | 11 |
| rejected | 11 | 69 |

*Table* 9.3  Percentage of good and bad candidates accepted and rejected, where the selection procedure has a validity of 0.25 and one-fifth of the candidates are accepted.

|  | good | bad |
|---|---|---|
| accepted | 6 | 14 |
| rejected | 14 | 66 |

tion, so it faces the same difficulties as the accuracy research described in Chapters 7 and 8 – that of finding a criterion. 'Success' in the Civil Service or the Navy is a very vague concept, and certain to be influenced by a lot else besides the candidate's real worth at the time of the assessment. None of the criteria used in interview research is entirely satisfactory. Vernon's CISSB research used ratings by the candidates' superiors after one year's work; the majority of the 426 early studies on personnel selection, reviewed by Dorcus and Jones (1950), used the same criterion. A rating or ranking or best/worst worker nomination is of course just an opinion, against which another opinion, that of the interviewer, is being compared. It could be argued that efficiency or success consist precisely in making a favourable impression on one's employer, if it were not that some employers, or their deputies who make their ratings, are likely to be unobservant, inconsistent, or biassed. Also, the candidate, even when safely past the selection board, will still be putting on a good front when supervisors and foremen are watching him. He is less likely to play the model employee before his workmates, which could explain why 'peer nominations' or 'buddy ratings' have proved surprisingly accurate at predicting success in army, navy and air force officers, salesmen and college students (Lewin and Zwany, 1976).

When selecting for the armed forces, or for college courses, it is possible to use training grades or final exam results as a criterion, bearing in mind that neither are perfectly reliable and both may be partly subjective. Studies in selecting salesmen often use sales figures as criterion, valid so long as the sales areas are comparable and the economic climate stays the same. Military studies sometimes use promotion as criterion; promotion depends on the promotion board's opinion of the worth of the candidates.

None of these criteria are very reliable, and this unreliability imposes necessary limits on validity; if the reliability of the foreman's ratings is only 0.75, the validity of the personnel manager's test and interview can't exceed 0.75. There is no way of predicting the unpredictable. Because criteria are unreliable, researchers prefer to use several, which also does better justice to the more complex type of job. Gardner and Williams's (1973) study of officer selection in the Royal Navy used six criteria: a rating of 'officer-like qualities' given at the end of basic training, two sets of marks for course work and three measures based on speed of promotion; some intercorrelated well, others poorly. Using multiple criteria which do not correlate well – and there would be little point in using more than one if they all pointed the same way – confuses the picture. Thus Gardner and Williams (1973) found that biographical data, such as leadership of societies at school, predicted, very weakly, speed of promotion, but not training grades, whereas a test of mechanical comprehension predicted training grades, but not speed of promotion. If the selection is being done on a sufficiently massive scale, the confusion might, in theory, be reduced by factor-analysing criterion and selection data.

Finding a criterion for a good naval officer or a good civil servant means deciding what makes a good naval officer or a good civil servant, which leads to all sort of profound questions well beyond the scope of this chapter. One should neither oversimplify by demanding a single criterion for something whose complexity obviously requires several, nor should one despair and conclude that because something can't be done perfectly, it shouldn't be done at all. While no criterion is perfect, some are sufficiently good to be worth using.

IMPROVING THE INTERVIEW

One could abolish the interview altogether, on the grounds that it wastes the candidates' time and tells the organization nothing about the candidates they couldn't discover from the application form, except what they look and sound like. One obstacle to abolition is the apparent fairness of the interview, especially when it is large and elaborate; many organizations' rules require them to interview five candidates even when they know quite well who they want. There are, however, some ways in which the interview's usefulness might be improved.

Ideally every selection team should collect the best criterion data they can on all the people they select, so they can continuously check how well they are doing. While 99 percent of American firms use interviews, 93 percent of them don't do anything to check on accuracy of selection. (A follow-up study is difficult if the firm doesn't have many employees, but in a small firm a bad choice will be more noticeable anyway.)

Some interviewers are better than others. Handyside and Duncan (1954) found that different interviewers had individual validity coefficients ranging from 0.17 to 0.66. Vernon and Parry (1949) found that one Wren[1] recruiting assistant had a personal validity coefficient of 0.55, whereas an objective test, superior to most interviewers, achieved only 0.39. The selectors themselves should be selected. Training schemes, which abound, have not yet been shown to be effective, but telling the interviewer what to look for, how to look for it, and how likely he is to miss it, can't be a bad idea. Interviewers can be warned of common sources of bias and inaccuracy – the tendency to make up one's mind too soon (Webster, 1964), the tendency to allow a previous succession of good or bad candidates to shift one's standard (Wexley et al., 1972), and the tendency to pay too much attention to the candidate's bad points (Constantin, 1976).

The interviewer who has a dozen items of information about a candidate is in the same position as the psychologist with nine MMPI scale scores (described in Chapter 3), and is as likely to use the information inefficiently – so advice on how to calculate a weighted average of the ratings of key aspects of the candidate's performance would be useful. (Although Dawes and Corrigan's (1974) analysis did suggest that an unweighted average could be used by the less-

[1]   Women's auxiliary branch of the Royal Navy.

numerate interviewer without losing much information.)

It has been argued that interviews are much better if the interviewer knows what he is looking for and reaches a number of specific decisions about the candidate's suitability. Yonge (1956) rated the attitudes of a number of employees to their work using a rating schedule and found that these correlated 0.70 with supervisors' ratings. A study on the US Navy found that interviewers could assess candidates' career motivation very well but didn't assess overall suitability very accurately.

Validity can be improved if the interviewer looks for specific items whose relevance has been established by follow-up studies. Vernon and Parry (1949) described lists of 'contra-indications'; the list for 'responsibility' included: unsteady, unprogressive or retrogressive work record, inability to give an intelligible account of own job, hypochondria, preference at school for handiwork, athletics, or geography over maths and science, underachievement at school. A candidate with more than a few of these signs was unlikely to be suitable for any responsible service job.

Research on survey interviewing has shown that some sorts of information are more trustworthy than others. People usually give accurate details of their social and economic status, and always report their sex correctly. Other information may be less reliable; in one study only half the candidates told the truth when asked if they had been to the 'Vocation Rehabilitation Agency', apparently afraid it would discourage the would-be employer. Intelligence and ability can be estimated reasonably accurately in the interviews, unlike most other traits (Mayfield, 1964).


## The psychiatric interview

The usual way of determining whether a person has a psychiatric illness is to ask him questions about the way he acts, thinks and feels; medical technology in the shape of blood tests, X-rays or urine analysis has little to offer the psychiatrist. (The principal aid to diagnosis, the personality test, is actually a formalization of the medical interview; questions like 'Do you often feel dizzy?', used in the Woodworth Personal Data Sheet of 1917 and its countless descendants, were borrowed from the psychiatric interview.) The psychiatrist gives a diagnosis, to indicate how the patient came to be ill, to predict what will happen to him, to choose a course of treatment, to help the efforts of any psychologists doing research in the clinic, and because it is required for the official statistics; he will probably use the disease categories devised by Kraepelin at the beginning of the century, subsequently elaborated and formalized by bodies like the World Health Organization.

The psychiatrist's problem is very similar to the selection interviewer's – trying to predict on the basis of a very limited encounter how someone is going to behave on a future occasion – but his task is made more difficult by having to use an unsatisfactory diagnostic system. On the other hand one could argue that his task is easier because his patient has less reason to conceal things than the candidate in an interview.

People who have great faith in the infallibility of doctors are often disturbed to find that psychiatric diagnosis is far from perfectly reliable; the evidence of reviews by Vernon (1964), Zubin (1967) and Ley (1972) is, however, clear enough. Most studies have tested inter-psychiatrist reliability – their ability to agree with each other about what the patient's diagnosis or treatment should be. Zubin summarized the evidence from six major studies. Agreement on major categories – organic brain disease, functional psychosis, neurosis or character disorder – ranged from 64 percent to 84 percent. Agreement within the major categories, on type of psychosis or neurosis, was lower, ranging from 38 percent to 66 percent. Zubin's opinion of these findings closely resembles Ulrich and Trumbo's comments on the reliability of selection interviewing: 'the degree of overall agreement between different observers with regard to specific diagnosis is too low for individual diagnosis.' Further evidence of the unreliability of diagnosis comes from studies of readmissions (Kendell, 1974) and of national differences in diagnostic rates (Leff, 1977).

The studies that Zubin reviewed didn't include a 'not ill at all' category; recent research suggests they should have. A widely cited recent study by Rosenhan (1973) showed that psychiatrists didn't detect people faking mild symptoms of schizophrenia; curiously enough 'buddy ratings' again proved very effective, for Rosenhan's 'pseudo-patients' were frequently spotted by the other patients. Spitzer an Endicott (1968) found that two psychiatrists who each interviewed twenty people with no history of psychiatric illness made only one 'not ill' diagnosis, and only four 'mildly ill' diagnoses. Psychiatrists seem to assume that anyone who presents himself for examination must have problems. McCoy (1976) confirmed this, finding that clinicians' assessments of children depended entirely on whether the parents said the child was difficult, regardless of how the child actually behaved. In fairness to psychiatrists and clinical psychologists, one should recall that various community surveys in Britain and the USA have shown that people with a perfectly clean bill of psychiatric health seem in a definite minority (Arthur, 1971). When the clinician is 'set' to look for signs of illness or health, as in psychiatric screening for the forces, he does rather better, predicting between 50 and 70 percent of future breakdowns correctly, with a 'false alarm' rate of around 5 percent.

The psychiatrist's job is made difficult for him by the deficiencies of the diagnostic system. According to the research of Beck *et al*. (1962) 62.5 percent of disagreements are caused by the system itself. Welner, Liss and Robins (1973) confirm this and describe a group of twenty-five undiagnosable patients, who either had too few symptoms to qualify for any of the American Psychiatric Association's categories, or so many that they fitted several equally well. 'Behavioural' interviewing is becoming popular; it abandons the diagnostic category as a mediating link between symptoms on the one hand, and treatment and likely future progress on the other, and concentrates on discovering just what the patient's problem is – how much an alcoholic drinks and how often – as a preliminary step to planning treatment (Miller, 1976).

The patient adds to the confusion by not telling one psychiatrist the same story he tells the other; in Beck *et al*.'s study this accounted for a further 5 percent of disagreements. For the rest, the blame lies with the psychiatrist himself for forgetting to ask about things, drawing the wrong conclusions from what he sees and hears, and adding up his data incorrectly. He can avoid these mistakes by employing a standard interview technique, such as the 'Present State Exam' (Wing *et al*., 1967).

## Conclusions

Both types of interview – selection and psychiatric – turn out to be very uncertain affairs, and it's very likely that the conclusions reached by other sorts of interviewers would turn out to be equally fallible. Some of the causes of this uncertainty are specific to the type of interview – the unhelpfulness of the diagnostic system in psychiatry and the interviewee's lack of any strong incentive to be honest in the selection interview – but others are common to both, and to other about another. The interviewer often isn't clear in his mind what he is looking for, or what he is trying to predict, and attempts to clarify his thoughts often lead to deep and almost unanswerable questions like 'What makes a good employee?' or 'What is mental health?'. If no one can agree about the qualities the interviewer is trying to predict, his task obviously becomes very difficult.

In a sense the interviewer is a victim of an oversimple trait model of personality. If one assumes that people's behaviour is produced by forces inside them, it makes sense to examine a person on one occasion, determine what traits he possesses, and then state confidently how he will behave on a completely different occasion. If, on the other hand, one assumes his behaviour is determined largely by where he is and who he's with, the interview doesn't look such a sensible enterprise. The same over-simple model of personality also assumes that people don't change, and don't react to experiences like being accepted or rejected for a job.

It is difficult to make any very constructive suggestions for allowing for the fallibility of decisions about other people. The psychiatrist can keep an open mind about the patient's diagnosis but he has to decide on a course of treatment, and has to decide when it's safe to let the patient out of hospital. The selection interviewer has even less scope for second thoughts; it's neither fair, nor necessarily even legal, to employ someone on trial and dismiss them if they don't prove suitable.

Interviewers are not alone in having to make irrevocable decisions about other people, nor are all such decisions 'professional' person perceptions. Virtually every decision made about someone else that is acted upon – and doesn't remain a private opinion – has consequences that can't be undone; deciding to get married is the most obvious case in point. It would be absurd to suggest that people shouldn't make decisions unless they can be certain they're going to be right, and it's arguably pointless even to enjoin caution; if decisions have to be made, but can't be assured of correctness, worrying about the outcome won't help.

# ACCURACY IN PERSON PERCEPTION

## Past, present and future issues

The history of research on accuracy of person perception has largely been a struggle to overcome methodological problems; while these have not been entirely solved, it is safe to say that researchers are now fully aware of their existence. Using these more refined methods it is possible to show that perceptions of other people are for the most part very inaccurate; this is as true of important decisions taken by trained experts as it is of the casual thoughts of the uninvolved observer. Further research on this point has little to offer. What is now required is some account of the abilities involved in perceiving others; only when this has been given is research on what makes or could make a 'good judge of others' likely to take some meaningful shape and cease to be an unhelpful mass of not particularly significant correlations. Given that so many opinions about other people turn out to be incorrect, perhaps the other issue most worth researching at present is what happens when one person misperceives another.

# BIBLIOGRAPHY

Adams-Webber, J.R. (1970) Elicited versus provided constructs in repertory grid technique: a review. *Brit. J. Soc. and Clin. Psychol.* *43*/349-53.

Adorno, T.W., Frenkel-Brunswick, E., Levinson, D.J. and Sanford R.N. (1950) *The Authoritarian Personality*. N.Y.: Harper and Row.

Allport, G.W. (1937) *Personality: a psychological interpretation*. N.Y.: Holt, Rinehart and Winston.

Allport, G.W. and Odbert, S, (1936) Trait names: a psycholexical study. *Psycholog. Monographs 47*, no. 221.

Altmann, H.A. and Shymko, D, (1970) A study of interpersonal judging accuracy as related to life style. *Western Psychologist 1*, 113-16.

Anastasi, A, (1976) *Psychological Testing* (4th ed.). N.Y.: Macmillan.

Anderson, N.H. (1965) Primacy effects in personality impression formation using a generalized order effect paradigm. *J. Personality and Soc. Psychol. 2*, 1-9.

Anderson, N.H. (1968) Likableness ratings of 555 personality-trait adjectives. *J. Personality and Soc. Psychol. 9*, 272-9.

Anderson, N.H. and Lopez L.L. (1974) Some psycholinguistic aspects of person perception. *Memory and Cognition 2*, 67-74.

Archer, D. and Akert, R.M. (1977) Words and everything else: verbal and non-verbal cues in social interpretation. *J. Personality and Soc. Psychol. 35*, 443-9.

Argyle, M. (1969) *Social Interaction*. London: Methuen.

Argyle, M. and Cook, M. (1976) *Gaze and Mutual Gaze*. Cambridge: Cambridge University Press.

Argyle, M. and Kendon, A. (1967) The experimental analysis of social performance in L. Berkowitz, (ed.) *Advances in Experimental Social Psychology, vol. 3*. N.Y.: Academic Press.

Argyle, M. and McHenry, R. (1971) Do spectacles really affect judgements of intelligence? *Brit. J. Soc. Clin. Psychol. 10*, 27-9.

Argyle, M., Alkema, F. and Gilmour, R. (1971) The communication of friendly and hostile attitudes by verbal and non-verbal signals. *Eur. J. Soc. Psychol. 1*, 385-402.

Argyle, M., Lefebvre, L. and Cook, M. (1974) The meaning of five patterns of gaze. *Eur. J. Soc. Psychol. 4*, 125-36.

Argyle, M., Salter, V., Nicholson, H.C., Williams, M. and Burgess, P. (1970) The communication of inferior and superior attitudes by verbal and non-verbal signals. *Brit. J. Soc. and Clin. Psychol. 9*, 222-31.

Arkin, R.M., Gleason, J.M. and Johnston, S. (1976) Effects of perceived choice, expected outcome and observed outcome of an action on the causal attributions of actions. *J. Exper. and Soc. Psychol. 12*, 151-8.

Arnheim, R. (1949) The Gestalt theory of expression. *Psycholog. Review 56*, 156-71.

Arthur, R.J. (1971) *An Introduction to Social Psychiatry*. Harmondsworth: Penguin.

Asch, S.E. (1946) Forming impressions of personality. *J. Abnormal and Soc. Psychol. 41*, 258-90.

Austin, J.L. (1961) *Sense and Sensibilia*. Oxford: Oxford University Press.

Babst, D., Gottfredson, D. and Ballard, K. (1968) Comparison of multiple regression and configural analysis techniques for developing base expectancy tables. *J. Res. in Crime and Delinquency 5*, 72-80.

Baker, B.O. and Sarbin. T.R. (1956) Differential mediation of social perception as a correlate of social adjustment. *Sociometry 19*, 69-83.

Balswick, J.O. and Anderson, J.A. (1968) Role definition in the unarranged date. *J. Marriage and the Family 31*, 776-8.

Bartlett, F.C. (1932) *Remembering: a study in experimental and social psychology*. Cambridge: Cambridge University Press.

Beck, A.P., Ward, C.H., Mendelson, M., Mock, J.E. and Erbaugh, J.K. (1962) Reliability of psychiatric diagnosis: 2. A study of the consistency of clinical judgements and ratings. *Am. J. Psychiatry 119*, 351-7.

Beckman, L. (1970) Effects of students' performance on teachers' and observers' attributions of causality. *J. Educ. Psychol. 61*, 76-82.

Bem, D.J. (1972) Self-perception theory, in L. Berkowitz (ed.) *Advances in Experimental Social Psychology*, vol. 6. N.Y.: Academic Press.

Benson, P.L., Karabenick, S.A. and Lerner, R.A. (1976) Pretty pleases: the effect of physical attractiveness, sex and race in receiving help. *J. Exper. Soc. Psychol. 12*, 409-14.

Berlew, D.E. and Williams, A.F. (1964) Interpersonal sensitivity under motive arousing conditions. *J. Abnormal and Soc. Psychol. 68*, 150-9.

Berscheid, E. and Walster, E.W. (1969) *Interpersonal Attraction*. Reading, Mass.: Addison-Wesley.

Bieri, J. (1966) Cognitive complexity and personality development, in O.J. Harvey (ed.) *Experience, Structure and Adaptability*. N.Y.: Springer.

Bieri, J., Atkins, A.L., Briar, S., Leaman, R.L., Miller, H. and Tripodi, T. (1966) *Clinical and Social Judgement: the discrimination of behavioural information*. N.Y.: Wiley.

Birdwhistell, R.L. (1968) Kinesics. *Internat. Encyclopedia of the Social Sciences 8*, 379-85.

Blake, R.R. and Ramsey, G.V. (1951) *Perception: an approach to personality*. N.Y.: Ronald Press.

Blanchard, W.A. (1966) Relevance of information and accuracy of interpersonal perception: a methodological note. *Psycholog. Reports 18*, 379-82.

Bonarius, J.C.J. (1965) Research in the personal construct theory of George A. Kelly, in B.A. Maher (ed.) *Progress in Experimental Personality Research, vol. 2*. N.Y.: Academic Press.

Borke, H. (1971) Interpersonal perception of young children: egocentrism or empathy. *Developmental Psychol. 5*, 263-9.

Borke, H. and Fiske, B.W. (1957) Factors influencing the prediction of behaviour from a diagnostic interview. *J. Consulting Psychol. 21*, 780-8.

Braginsky, B.M. and Braginsky, D.D. (1967) Schizophrenic patients in the psychiatric interview: an experimental study of their effectiveness at manipulation. *J. Consulting Psychol. 31*, 543-7.

Brigham, J.C. (1971) Ethnic stereotypes. *Psycholog. Bull. 76*, 15-38.

Bronfenbrenner, U., Harding, J. and Gallway, M. (1958) The measure of skill in social perception, in D.C. McClelland (ed.) *Talent and Society*. N.Y.: van Nostrand Reinhold.

Brown, R. (1965) *Social Psychology*. London: Collier MacMillan.

Bruner, J.S. (1957) On perceptual readiness. *Psycholog. Review 64*, 123-52.

Bruner, J.S. Goodnow, J.L. and Austin, G.A. (1956) *A Study of*

*Thinking*. N.Y.: Wiley.

Bruner, J.S., Shapiro, D., and Tagiuri, R. (1958) The meaning of traits in isolation and in combination, in R. Tagiuri and L. Petrullo (eds.) *Person Perception and Interpersonal Behaviour*. Stanford, Calif.: Stanford U.P.

Buchanan, B.A. and Bruning, J.L. (1971) Connotative meanings of first names and nicknames on three dimensions. *J. Soc. Psychol.* 85, 143-4.

Buck, R. (1976) A test of non-verbal receiving ability: preliminary studies. *Human Communication Res.* 2, 162-71.

Buck, R., Miller, R.E. and Caul, W.F. (1974) Sex, personality and physiological variables in the communication of emotion via facial expression. *J. Personality and Soc. Psychol.* 30, 587-96.

Bugenthal, D.E. (1974) Interpretations of naturally occurring discrepancies between words and intonation: modes of inconsistency resolution. *J. Personality and Soc. Psychol.* 30, 125-33.

Byrne, D. and Blaylock, B. (1963) Similarity and assumed similarity of attitudes between husbands and wives. *J. Abnormal and Soc. Psychol.* 67, 636-40.

Campbell, D.T. (1967) Stereotypes and the perception of group differences. *Am. Psychologist* 22, 817-29.

Campbell, J.P. and Dunnette, M.D. (1968) Effectiveness of T-group experiences in managerial training and development. *Psycholog. Bull.* 70, 73-104.

Cantor, J.H. (1976) Individual needs and salient constructs in interpersonal perception. *J. Personality and Soc. Psychol.* 34, 519-25.

Cattell, R.B. (1937) Measurement versus intuition in applied psychology. *Character and Personality* 6, 114-31.

Cattell, R.B. (1946) *Description and Measurement of Personality*. Yonkers, N.Y.: World Book Co.

Chaikin, A.L. and Darley, J.M. (1973) Victim or perpetrator: defensive attribution of responsibility and the need for order and justice. *J. Personality and Soc. Psychol.* 25, 268-75.

Chance, J.E. and Meaders, W. (1960) Needs and interpersonal perception. *J. Personality* 28, 200-9.

Chapman, L.J. and Chapman, J.P. (1967) Genesis of popular but erroneous psycho-diagnostic observations. *J. Abnormal Psychol.* 73, 193-204.

Christensen, L. (1970) Validity of person perception accuracy scores. *Perceptual and Motor Skills* 30, 871-7.

Clements, W.H. (1967) Marital interaction and marital stability: a point of view and a descriptive comparison of stable and unstable marriages. *J. Marriage and the Family 29*, 697-702.

Cline, V.B. (1964) Interpersonal perception, in B.A. Maher (ed.) *Progress in Experimental Personality Research, vol. 1.* N.Y.: Academic Press.

Cline, V.B. and Richards, J.M. (1960) Accuracy of interpersonal perception – a general trait. *J. Abnormal and Soc. Psychol. 60*, 1-7.

Cobin, M.T. and McIntyre, L.J. (1961) *The Development and Application of a New Method to Test the Relative Effectiveness of Specific Visual Production Techniques for Instructional Television.* Urbana, Ill.: University of Illinois Press.

Cohen, E. (1953) The methodology of Notcutt and Silva's 'Knowledge of other people': a critique. *J. Abnormal and Soc. Psychol. 48.*

Cohen, S.L. and Bunker, K.A. (1975) Subtle effects of sex-role stereotypes on recruiters' hiring decisions. *J. Applied Psychol. 60*, 566-72.

Colby, K.M. (1977) Appraisal of four psychological theories of paranoid phenomena. *J. Abnormal Psychol. 86*, 54-9.

Collins, B.E. (1974) Four components of the Rotter Internal External Scale: belief in a difficult world, a just world, a predictable world, and a politically responsive world. *J. Personality and Soc. Psychol. 29*, 381-91.

Comfort, A. (1971) The likelihood of human pheromones. *Nature 230*, 432-3, 479.

Conklin, R.C. and Ogston, D.G. (1970) The effect of varying the mode of information on interpersonal judging accuracy. *Western Psychologist 1*, 100-5.

Constantin, S.W. (1976) An investigation of information favourability in the employment interview. *J. Applied Psychol. 61*, 743-9.

Cook, M. and Smith, J.M.C. (1974) Group ranking techniques in the study of the accuracy of person perception. *Brit. J. Psychol. 65*, 427-35.

Cook, M. and Smith, J.M.C. (1975) The role of gaze in impression formation. *Brit. J. Soc. and Clin. Psychol. 14*, 19-25.

Cooper, J., Jones, E.E. and Tuller, S.M. (1972) Attribution, dissonance and the illusion of uniqueness. *J. Exper. Soc. Psychol. 8*, 45-7.

Corsini, R.J. (1956) Understanding and similarity in marriage. *J. Abnormal and Soc. Psychol. 52*, 327-32.

Coursey, R.D. (1973) Clothes doth make the man, in the eye of the beholder. *Perceptual and Motor Skills 36*, 1259-64.

Crockett, W.H. (1965) Cognitive complexity and impression formation, in B.A. Maher (ed.) *Progress in Experimental Personality Research, vol. 2.* N.Y.: Academic Press.

Cronbach, L.J. (1955) Processes affecting scores on 'understanding of others' and assumed similarity. *Psycholog. Bull. 52*, 177-93.

Cronbach, L.J. (1960) *Essentials of Psychological Testing* (2nd ed.). N.Y.: Harper and Row.

Cronbach, L.J. (1970) *Essentials of Psychological Testing* (3rd ed.). N.Y.: Harper and Row.

Crow, W.J. (1957) The effects of training upon accuracy and variability in interpersonal perception. *J. Abnormal and Soc. Psychol. 55*, 355-9.

Crow, W.J. and Hammond, K.R. (1957) The generality of accuracy and response sets in interpersonal perception. *J. Abnormal and Soc. Psychol. 54*, 384-90.

Dailey, C.A. (1963) An experimental method for improving interpretation and understanding. *Psycholog. Reports 13*, 240.

Darwin, C. (1872) *The Expression of the Emotions in Man and Animals.* London: John Murray.

Davis, W.L. and Davis, D.E. (1972) Internal-external control and attribution of responsibility for success and failure. *J. Personality 40*, 123-36.

Davitz, J.R. (1964) *The Communication of Emotional Meaning.* N.Y.: McGraw-Hill.

Dawes, R.M. and Corrigan, B. (1974) Linear models in decision making. *Psycholog. Bull. 81*, 95-106.

De Charms, R., Carpenter, V. and Kuperman, A. (1965) The 'Origin – Pawn' variable in person perception. *Sociometry 28*, 241-58.

Deci, E.L. (1971) Effects of externally mediated rewards on intrinsic motivation. *J. Personality and Soc. Psychol. 18*, 105-15.

DeSoto, C., Keuthe, J.L. and Wunderlich, R. (1960) Social perception and self perception of high and low authoritarians. *J. Soc. Psychol. 52*, 149-55.

Dienstbier, R.A. and Munter, P.O. (1971) Cheating as a function of the labelling of natural arousal. *J. Personality and Soc. Psychol. 17*, 213-18.

Dion, K.K. (1972) Physical attractiveness and valuations of children's transgressions. *J. Personality and Soc. Psychol. 24*, 207-13.

Dorcus, R.M. and Jones, M.H. (1950) *Handbook of Employee Selection*. N.Y.: McGraw-Hill.

Dornbusch, S.M., Hastorf, A.H., Richardson, S.A., Muzzy, R.E. and Vreeland, R.S. (1965) The perceiver and perceived: their relative influence on categories of interpersonal perception. *J. Personality and Soc. Psychol. 1*, 434-30.

Dymond, R.F. (1949) A scale for the measurement of empathic ability. *J. Consulting Psychol. 13*, 127-33.

Dymond, R.F. (1950) Personality and empathy. *J. Consulting Psychol. 14*, 343-50.

Dymond, R.F. (1954) Interpersonal perception and marital happiness. *Canadian J. Psychol. 8*, 164-71.

Dymond, R.F. Hughes, A.S. and Raabe, V.L. (1952) Measurable changes in empathy with age. *J. Consulting Psychol. 16*, 202-6.

Ekman, P. (1972) Universals and cultural differences in facial expressions of emotion, in J. Cole (ed.) *Nebraska Symposium on Motivation*. Lincoln, Nebraska: University of Nebraska Press.

Ekman, P. and Friesen, W.V. (1969) Origin, usage and coding: the basis of five categories in non-verbal behaviour. *Semiotica 1*, 49-98.

Ellsworth, P.C., Carlsmith, J. and Henson, A. (1972) The stare as a stimulus to flight in human subjects: a series of field experiments. *J. Personality and Soc. Psychol. 21*, 302-11.

Engelmann, W. (1928) Zur Psychologie des ersten blickes: Intelligenz und Tauglichkeitsschatzung in Buchdrucklehrlingen. *Industrielle Psychotechnik 10*, 307-10.

Estes, S.C. (1938) Judging personality from expressive behaviour. *J. Abnormal and Soc. Psychol. 33*, 217-36.

Exline, R.V. (1957) Group climate as a factor in the relevance and accuracy of social perception. *J. Abnormal and Soc. Psychol. 55*, 382-8.

Exline, R.V. (1971) Visual interaction: the glances of power and preference, in J.K. Cole (ed.) *Nebraska Symposium on Motivation*. Lincoln, Nebraska: University of Nebraska Press.

Exline, R.V. and Yellin, A. (1969) Eye contact as a sign between man and monkey. *Proceedings of the 19th International Congress on Psychology*, London.

Exline, R.V., Thibaut, J., Hickey, C.B. and Gumpert, P. (1970) Visual interaction in relation in Machiavellianism and an unethical act. In R. Christie and F.L. Geis (eds) *Studies in Machiavellianism*. N.Y.: Academic Press.

Eysenck, H.J. (1967) *The Biological Basis of Personality*. Springfield, Ill.: C.C. Thomas.

Eysenck, H.J. (1970) *The Structure of Human Personality* (3rd ed.). London: Methuen.

Eysenck, H.J. and Crown, S. (1948) National stereotypes: an experimental and methodological study. *Internat. J. Opinion and Attitude Res. 2*, 26-39.

Eysenck, S.B.G. (1962) The validity of a personality questionnaire as determined by the method of nominated groups. *Life Sciences 1*, 13-18.

Fancher, R.E. (1966) Explicit personality theories and accuracy in person perception. *J. Personality 34*, 252-61.

Fancher, R.E. (1967) Accuracy versus validity in person perception. *J. Consulting Psychol. 31*, 264-7.

Fancher, R.E. (1969) Group and individual accuracy in person perception. *J. Consulting Psychol. 33*, 127.

Feather, N.T. (1969) Attribution of responsibility and valence of success and failure in relation to initial confidence and task performance. *J. Personality and Soc. Psychol. 13*, 129-44.

Feldman-Summers, S. and Kiesler, S.B. (1974) Those who are number two try harder: the effect of sex on attributions of causality. *J. Personality and Soc. Psychol. 30*, 846-55.

Feleky, A.M. (1914) The expression of emotions. *Psycholog. Review 21*, 33-41.

Festinger, L. and Carlsmith, J.M. (1959) Cognitive consequences of forced compliance. *J. Abnormal and Soc. Psychol. 58*, 203-11.

Fishbein, M. and Ajzen, I. (1973) Attribution of responsibility: a theoretical note. *J. Exper. Soc. Psychol. 9*, 148-53.

Fiske, D.W. (1974) The limits for a conventional science of personality. *J. Personality 42*, 1-11.

Friendly, M.I. and Glucksberg, S. (1970) On the description of subcultural lexicons: a multi-dimensional approach. *J. Personality and Soc. Psychol. 14*, 55-65.

Frijda, N.A. (1958) Facial expression and situational cues. *J. Abnormal and Soc. Psychol. 57*, 149-55.

Frijda, N.A. (1969) Recognition of emotion, in L. Berkowitz (ed.) *Advances in Experimental Social Psychology, vol. 4*. N.Y.: Academic Press.

Gabennesch, H. and Hunt, L.L. (1971) The relative accuracy of interpersonal perception of high and low authoritarians. *J. Exper.*

*Res. in Personality 5*, 43-8.

Gage, N.L. (1952) Judging interests from expressive behaviour. *Psycholog. Monographs 66*, no. 18 (Whole no. 350).

Gardner, K.E. and Williams, A.P.O. (1973) A twenty-five year follow-up of an extended interview selection procedure in the Royal Navy. *Occupational Psychol. 47*, 1-13.

Gibbins, K. (1969) Communication aspects of women's clothes and their relation to fashionability. *Brit. J. Soc. and Clin. Psychol. 8*, 301-12.

Giedt, F.H. (1955) Comparison of visual, content and auditory cues in interviewing. *J. Consulting Psychol. 19*, 407-16.

Gilbert, G.M. (1951) Stereotype persistence and change among college students. *J. Abnormal and Soc. Psychol. 46*, 245-54.

Godfrey, B.W. and Lowe, C.A. (1975) Devaluation of innocent victims: an attributional analysis with the just world paradigm. *J. Personality and Soc. Psychol. 31*, 944-51.

Goffman, E. (1956) *The Presentation of Self in Everyday Life*. Edinburgh: Edinburgh University Press.

Goldberg, L.R. (1965) Diagnosticians vs diagnostic signs: the diagnosis of psychosis vs neurosis from the MMPI. *Psycholog. Monographs 79*, no. 9 (Whole no. 602).

Goldberg, L.R. (1970) Man versus model of man: a rationale, plus some evidence, for a method of improving clinical inferences. *Psycholog. Bull. 73*, 422-32.

Gollin, E.S. (1954) Forming impressions of personality. *J. Personality 23*, 65-76.

Gough, H.G. (1948) A sociological theory of psychopathy. *Am. J. Sociol. 53*, 359-66.

Gough, H.G. (1962) Clinical vs statistical prediction in psychology in L. Postman (ed.) *Psychology in the Making*. N.Y.: Knopf.

Gough, H.G. and Petersen, D.R. (1952) The identification and measurement of predispositional factors in crime and delinquency. *J. Consulting Psychol. 16*, 207-12.

Graham, J.R. (1971) Feedback and accuracy of predictions of hospitalisations from the MMPI. *J. Clin. Psychol. 27*, 243-5.

Gray, C.W., Barnes, C.B. and Wilkins, E.E. (1965) The process of prediction as a function of the correlation between two scaled variables. *Psychonomic Science 3*, 231-2.

Guiora, A. (1965) On clinical diagnosis and prediction. *Psycholog. Reports 17*, 779-84.

Haggard, F.A. and Isaacs, K.S. (1966) Micromomentary facial expressions as indicators of ego mechanisms in psychotherapy, in L.A. Gottschalk and A.H. Auerbach (eds.) *Methods of Research in Psychotherapy.* N.Y.: Appleton-Century-Crofts.

Hall, E.T. (1966) *The Hidden Dimension.* N.Y.: Doubleday.

Handyside, J.D. and Duncan, D.C. (1954) Four years later: a follow-up on an experiment in selecting superiors. *Occupational Psychol. 28,* 9-23.

Harris, J.G. (1972) Prediction of success on a distant Pacific island, Peace Corps style. *J. Consulting and Clin. Psychol. 38,* 181-90.

Hart, H. (1923) Predicting parole success. *J. Criminal Law and Criminology 14,* 405-13.

Hartshorne, H. and May, M.A. (1928) *Studies in Deceit.* N.Y.: Macmillan.

Hastorf, A.H. and Bender, I.E. (1952) A caution respecting the measurement of empathic ability. *J. Abnormal and Soc. Psychol. 47,* 574-6.

Hatch, R.S., (1962), *An Evaluation of a Forced Choice Differential Accuracy Approach to the Measurement of Supervisors' Empathy.* Englewood Cliffs, N.J.: Prentice Hall.

Heider, F. (1958) *The Psychology of Interpersonal Relations.* N.Y.: Wiley.

Helfand, I. (1956) Role taking in schizophrenia. *J. Consulting Psychol. 20,* 37-41.

Hess, E.H. (1965) Attitude and pupil size. *Scientific American 212,* 46-54.

Hewitt, L.E. (1958) Student perceptions of traits desired in themselves as dating and marriage partners. *Marriage and Family Living 20,* 344-9.

Hillman, J.S. (1974) An analysis of male and female roles in two periods of children's literature. *J. Educ. Res. 68,* 84-8.

Hirshman, R. (1975) Cross-model effects of anticipatory bogus heart-rate feedback in a negative emotional context. *J. Personality and Soc. Psychol. 31,* 13-19.

Hobson, G.N., Strongman, K.T., Bull, D. and Craig, G. (1973) Anxiety and gaze aversion in dyadic encounters. *Brit. J. Soc. and Clin. Psychol. 12,* 122-9.

Hoffman, M.L. (1977) Sex differences in empathy and related behaviour. *Psycholog. Bull. 84,* 712-22.

Hoffman, P.J., Slovic, P., and Rorer, L.G. (1968) An analysis of variance model for the assessment of configural cue utilisation in clinical judgement. *Psycholog. Bull. 69*, 338-49.

Hollingworth, H.L. (1916) *Vocational Psychology*. N.Y.: Appleton-Century-Crofts.

Jackson, E.D. and Potkay, C.R. (1973) Pre-college influence on sexual experience in co-eds. *J. Sex Res. 9*, 143-9.

Jahoda, G. (1963) Refractive errors, intelligence and social mobility. *Brit. J. Soc. and Clin. Psychol. 1*, 96-106.

Jecker, J.D., Maccoby, N. and Breitrose, H.S. (1965) Improving accuracy in interpreting non-verbal cues of comprehension. *Psychol. in the School 2*, 239-44.

Johnson, T.J., Feigenbaun, R. and Weib, M. (1964) Some determinants and consequences of the teacher's perception of causality. *J. Educ. Psychol. 55*, 237-46.

Jones, E.E. and Davis, K.E. (1965) From acts to dispositions: the attribution process in person perception, in L. Berkowitz (ed.) *Advances in Experimental Social Psychology, vol. 2*. N.Y.: Academic Press.

Jones, E.E. and Harris, V.A. (1967) The attribution of attitudes, *J. Exper. Soc. Psychol. 3*, 1-24.

Jones, E.E. and Nisbett, R.E. (1971) The actor and the observer: divergent perceptions of the causes of behaviour, in E.E. Jones, D.E. Kanouse, H.H. Kelley, R.E. Nisbett, S. Valins and B. Weiner (eds.) *Attribution: perceiving the causes of behaviour*. Morristown, N.J.: General Learning Press.

Jones, E.E., Kanouse, D.E., Kelley, H.H., Nisbett, R.E., Valins, S. and Weiner, B. (eds.) (1971) *Attribution: perceiving the causes of behaviour*. Morristown, N.J.: General Learning Press.

Jones, E.E. Kanouse, D.E. Kelley, H.H. Nisbett, R.E., Valins, S. and Weiner, B. (eds.) (1971) *Attribution: perceiving the causes of behaviour*. Morristown, N.J.: General Learning Press.

Kahn, R.L. and Cannell, C.F. (1957) *The Dynamics of Interviewing*. N.Y.: Wiley.

Kahneman, D. and Tversky, (1973) On the psychology of prediction. *Psycholog. Review 80*, 237-51.

Karniol, R. and Ross, M. (1976) The development of causal attributions in social perception. *J. Personality and Soc. Psychol. 34*, 455-

Katz, D. and Braly, K. (1933) Racial stereotypes of one hundred college students. *J. Abnormal and Soc. Psychol. 28*, 280-90.

Kelley, H.H. (1950) The warm-cold variable in first impressions of persons. *J. Personality 18*, 431-9.

Kelley, H.H. (1967) Attribution theory in social psychology, in D. Levine (ed.) *Nebraska Symposium on Motivation*. Lincoln, Nebraska: University of Nebraska Press.

Kellogg, R. and Baron, R.S. (1975) Attribution theory, insomnia and the reverse placebo effect: a reversal of Storms and Nisbett's findings. *J. Personality and Soc. Psychol. 32*, 231-6.

Kelly, G.A. (1955) *The Psychology of Personal Constructs*. N.Y.: Norton.

Kendell, R.E. (1974) The stability of psychiatric diagnosis. *Brit. J. Psychiatry 124*, 352-6.

Kendon, A. (1970) Movement co-ordination in social interaction: some examples considered. *Acta Psychologica 32*, 101-25.

Kendon, A. (1972) Some relationships between body motion and speech, in A. Siegman and B. Pope (eds) *Studies in Dyadic Interaction*. N.Y.: Pergamon.

Kenny, C.T. and Fletcher, D. (1973) Effects of beardedness on person perception. *Perceptual and Motor Skills 37*, 413-14.

Kirkpatrick, C. and Hobart, C. (1954) Disagreement, disagreement estimate and non-empathic imputation for intimacy groups varying from favourite date to married. *Am. Sociolog. Review 19*, 10-9.

Kleinmuntz, B. (1963) Profile analysis revisited: a heuristic approach. *J. Counselling Psychol. 10*, 315-21.

Koeske, R.K. and Koeske, G.F. (1975) An attributional approach to moods and the menstrual cycle. *J. Personality and Soc. Psychol. 31*, 473-8.

Kramer, E. (1963) Judgements of personal characteristics and emotions from non-verbal aspects of speech. *Psycholog. Bull. 55*, 148-70.

Krasner, L. (1958) Studies of the verbal conditioning of behaviour. *Psycholog. Bull. 55*, 148-70.

Krause, M.S. (1961) The measurement of transitory anxiety. *Psycholog. Review 68*, 178-89.

Krech, D., Crutchfield, R.S. and Ballachey, E.L. (1962) *Individual in Society*. N.Y.: McGraw-Hill.

Krout, M.H. (1954) An experimental attempt to determine the significance of unconscious manual symbolic movements. *J. Genetic Psychol. 51*, 121-52.

Kuusinen, J. (1969) Affective and denotative structures of personality ratings. *J. Personality and Soc. Psychol. 12*, 181-8.

Laing, R.D., Phillipson, H. and Lee, A.R. (1966) *Interpersonal Perception*. London: Tavistock.

Lampel, A.K. and Anderson, N.H. (1968) Combining visual and verbal information in an impression formation task. *J. Personality and Soc. Psychol. 9*, 1-6.

Landis, C. (1929) Studies of emotional reactions: III. General behaviour and facial expressions. *J. Comparative Psychol. 4*, 447-509.

Landy, F.J. (1976) The validity of the interview in police officer selection. *J. Applied Psychol. 61*, 193-7.

Langfeld, J.S. (1918) Judgements of facial expression and suggestion. *Psycholog. Review 25*, 488-94.

Lawson, E.D. (1971) Hair colour, personality and the observer. *Psycholog. Reports 28*, 311-22.

Lay, C.H. and Jackson, D.N. (1969) Analysis of the generality of trait-inferential relationships. *J. Personality and Soc. Psychol. 12*, 12-21.

Le Compte, W.F. and Rosenfeld, H.M. (1971) Effects of minimal eye contact in the instruction period on impressions of the experimenter. *J. Exper. Soc. Psychol. 7*, 211-20.

Leff, J. (1977) International variations in the diagnosis of psychiatric illness. *Brit. J. Psychiatry 131*, 329-38.

Lerner, M.J. (1965) Evaluation of a performance as a function of the performer's reward and attractiveness. *J. Personality and Soc. Psychol. 4*, 203-10.

Lerner, M.J. and Simmons, C.H. (1966) Observer's reaction to the 'innocent victim' – compassion or rejection? *J. Personality and Soc. Psycho. 4*, 203-10.

Levenson, H. (1972) Distinctions within the concept of internal-external control: development of a new scale. *Proceedings of the Annual Convention of the American Psychological Association, 1972, 7*, 261-2.

Lewin, A.Y. and Zwany, A. (1976) Peer nominations: a model, literature critique and a paradigm for research. *Personnel Psychol. 29*, 423-47.

Ley, P. (1972) Acute psychiatric patients, in P. Mittler (ed.) *The Assessment of Physical and Mental Handicap*. London: Methuen.

Liberman, P. (1965) On the acoustic basis of the perception of intonation by linguists. *Word 21*, 40-54.

Lindgren, H.C. and Robinson, J. (1953) An evaluation of Dymond's test of insight and empathy. *J. Consulting Psychol. 17*, 172-6.

Lindzey, G. (1965) Seer versus sign. *J. Exper. Res. in Personality 1*, 17-26.

Lippman, W. (1922) *Public Opinion.* N.Y.: Harcourt Brace.

Little, B. (1969) Sex differences and comparability of three measures of cognitive complexity. *Psycholog. Reports 24*, 607-9.

Luchins, A.S. (1957) Experimental attempts to minimize the impact of first impressions in C. Hovland (ed.) *The Order of Presentation in Persuasion.* New Haven, Conn.: Yale University Press.

Luginbuhl, J.E.R., Crowe, D.A. and Kahan, J.P. (1975) Causal attributions for success and failure. *J. Personality and Soc. Psychol. 31*, 86-93.

McArthur, L.Z. and Post, D.L. (1977) Figural emphasis and person perception. *J. Exper. Soc. Psychol. 13*, 520-35.

Maccoby, E.E. and Jacklin C.N. (1975) *The Psychology of Sex Differences.* Stanford, Calif.: Stanford University Press.

McCoy, S.A. (1976) Clinical judgements of normal childhood behaviour. *J. Consulting and Clin. Psychol. 44*, 710-14.

McHenry, R.E. (1971) New methods of assessing the accuracy of interpersonal perception. *J. the Theory of Soc. Behaviour 1*, 109-19.

McKeachie, W. (1952) Lipstick as a determiner of first impressions of personality: an experiment for the general psychology course. *J. Soc. Psychol. 36*, 241-4.

McKillip, J. and Posavac, E.J. (1972) Attribution of responsibility for an accident: effects of similarity to the victim and severity of consequences. *Proceedings of the Annual Convention of the American Psychological Association, 1972, 7*, 181-2.

Magson, E.H. (1926) How we judge intelligence. *Brit. J. Psychol. Monograph Supplement 3*, 9.

Maier, N.R.F. and Thurber, J.A. (1968) Accuracy of judgements of deception when an interview is watched, heard and read. *Personnel Psychology 21*, 23-30.

Mann, J.W. (1967) Inconsistent thinking about groups and individual. *J. Soc. Psychol. 71*, 235-45.

Mannheim, M.D. and Wilkins, C.T. (1955) *Prediction methods in Relation to Borstal Training.* London: HMSO.

Maselli, M.D. and Altrocchi, T. (1969) Attribution of intent. *Psycholog. Bull. 71*, 445-54.

Matarazzo, J.D. and Saslow, G. (1961) Differences in interview interaction behaviour among normal and deviant groups, in C.A. Berg and C.M. Bass (eds) *Conformity and Deviation*. N.Y.: Harper and Row.

Mayfield, E.C. (1964) The selection interview: a re-evaluation of published research. *Personnel Psychol. 17*, 239-60.

Meehl, P.E. (1954) *Clinical versus Statistical Prediction*. Minneapolis, Minn.: University of Minnesota Press.

Meehl, P.E. (1959) A comparison of clinicans with five statistical methods of identifying psychotic MMPI profiles. *J. Counselling Psychol. 6*, 102-9.

Meehl, P.E. (1961) Logic for the clinican: review of T. Sarbin, R. Taft and D. Bailey's 'Clinical inference and cognitive theory'. *Contemp. Psychol. 7*, 389-91.

Meehl, P.E. and Rosen, A. (1955) Antecedent probability and the efficiency of psychometric signs, patterns or cutting scores. *Psycholog. Bull. 52*, 194-216.

Mehrabian, A. and Ferris, S.R. (1967) Inference of attitudes from non-verbal communication in two channels. *J. Consulting Psychol. 31*, 248-52.

Mehrabian, A. and Wiener, M. (1967) Decoding of inconsistent communication. *J. Personality and Soc. Psychol. 6*, 109-14.

Milgram, N.A. (1960) Cognitive and empathetic factors in role taking by schizophrenic and brain-damaged patients. *J. Abnormal and Soc. Psychol. 60*, 219-24.

Milgram, S. (1963) Behavioural study of obedience. *J. Abnormal and Soc. Psychol. 67*, 371-8.

Miller, A.G. (1970) Role of physical attractiveness in impression formation. *Psychonomic Science 19*, 241-3.

Miller, A.G., Gillen, B., Schenker, C. and Radlove, S. (1974) The prediction and perception of obedience to authority. *J. Personality 42*, 23-42.

Miller, D.T. and Ross, M., (1975) Self-serving biases in the attribution of causality: fact or fiction? *Psycholog. Bull. 82*, 213-25.

Miller, R.L., Brickman, P. and Bolen, D. (1975) Attribution versus persuasion as a means for modifying behaviour. *J. Personality and Soc. Psychol.*

Miller, W.R. (1976) Alcoholism scales and objective assessment methods: a review. *Psycholog. Bull. 83*, 649-74.

Miron, M.S. (1969) What is it that is being differentiated by the semantic differential? *J. Personality and Soc. Psychol. 12*, 189-93.

Mischel, W. (1968) *Personality and Assessment*. N.Y.: Wiley.

Monson, T.C. and Snyder, M. (1977) Actors, observers and the attribution process: toward a reconceptualization. *J. Exper. Soc. Psychol. 13*, 89-111.

Morin, R.E. Knoick, A., Troxell, N. and McPherson, S. (1965) Information and reaction time for 'naming' responses. *J. Exper. Psychol. 70*, 309-14.

Mulaik, S.T. (1964) Are personality factors raters' conceptual factors. *J. Consulting Psychol. 28*, 506-11.

Munn, N.L. (1940) The effect of knowledge of situation upon judgement of emotion from facial expressions. *J. Abnormal and Soc. Psychol. 35*, 324-38.

Murphy, G.E. (1972) Clinical identification of suicide risk. *Archives of General Psychiatry, 27*, 356-9.

Murray, H.A. (1933) The effect of fear upon estimates of the maliciousness of other personalities. *J. Soc. Psychol. 4*, 310-29.

Murstein, B.I. (1972) Person perception and courtship progress among premarital couples. *J. Marriage and the Family 34*, 621-6.

Murstein, B.I. and Beck, G.D. (1972) Person perception, marriage adjustment and social desirability. *J. Consulting and Clin. Psychol. 39*, 396-403.

Murstein, B.I. and Pryer, R.S. (1959) The concept of projection: a review. *Psycholog. Bull. 56*, 353-74.

Nicholls, J.G. (1975) Causal attributions and other achievement-related cognitions: effects of task outcome, attainment value and sex. *J. Personality and Social Psychol. 31*, 379-89.

Nisbett, R.E., Caputo, C., Legant, P. and Maracek, J. (1973) Behaviour as seen by the actor and as seen by the observer. *J. Personality and Soc. Psychol. 27*, 154-65.

Nisbett, R.E., Crandall, R., Borgida, E. and Reed, H. (1976) Popular induction: information is not necessarily informative, in J. Carroll and J. Payne (eds) *Cognition and Social Behaviour*. Potomac, Md.: Erlbaum.

Norman, W.T. (1963) Toward an adequate taxonomy of personality attributes: replicated factor structure in peer nomination personality ratings. *J. Abnormal and Soc. Psychol. 66*, 574-83.

Nottcutt, B. and Silva, A.L.M. (1951) Knowledge of other people. *J. Abnormal and Soc. Psychol. 46*, 30-7.

Nystedt, L. and Magnusson, D. (1972) Predictive efficiency as a function of amount of information. *Multivariate Behavioural Res. 7*, 441-50.

Oldfield, R.C. (1939) Some verbal problems connected with character nomenclature. *J. Mental Science 83*, 245-55.

O'Neal, E. (1971) Influence of future choice importance and arousal upon the halo effect. *J. Personality and Soc. Psychol. 19*, 334-40.

Osgood, C.E., Suci, C.J. and Tannenbaum, R.H. (1957) *The Measurement of Meaning*. Urbana, Ill.: University of Illinois Press.

Oskamp, S. (1962) The relationship of clinical experience and training methods to several criteria of clinical prediction. *Psycholog. Monographs 76*, no. 28 (Whole no. 547).

Parkinson, C.N. (1958) *Parkinson's Law, or the Pursuit of Progress*. London: John Murray.

Passini, F.T. and Norman, W.T. (1966) A universal conception of personality structure. *J. Personality and Soc. Psychol. 4*, 44-9.

Peabody, D. (1967) Trait inferences: evaluative and descriptive aspects. *J. Personality and Soc. Psychol.*, *Monograph Supplement 7*, no. 4 (Whole no. 644).

Porter, E.R., Argyle, M. and Salter, V. (1970) What is signalled by proximity? *Perceptual and Motor Skills 30*, 39-42.

Pritchard, D.A. (1977) Linear versus configural statistical prediction. *J. Consulting and Clin. Psychol. 45*, 559-63.

Rabinowitz, N. (1956) A note on the social perceptions of authoritarians and non-authoritarians. *J. Abnormal and Soc. Psychol. 53*, 384-6.

Raymond, B.J. and Unger, R.K. (1972) 'The apparel oft proclaims the man': co-operation with deviant and conventional youths. *J. Soc. Psychol. 87*, 75-82.

Reid, T. (1764) *Essays on the Intellectual Powers of Man*. Edinburgh: Bell.

Remmers, H.H. (1950) A quantitative index of social-psychological empathy. *Am. J. Orthopsychiatry 20*, 161-5.

Rodin, M.J. (1972) The informativeness of trait descriptions. *J. Personality and Social Psychol. 21*, 341-4.

Rorer, L.G., Hoffman, P.J., Dickman, H.R., and Slovic, P. (1967) Configural judgements revealed. *Proceedings of the Annual Convention of the American Psychological Association*.

Rosen, B. and Jerdee, T.H. (1974) Effects of applicant's sex and difficulty of job on evaluations of candidates for managerial positions. *J. Applied Psychol. 59*, 511-12.

Rosenberg, S. and Jones, R. (1972) A method for investigating and representing a person's implicit theory of personality: Theodore Dreiser's view of people. *J. Personality and Soc. Psychol. 22*, 372-86.

Rosenberg, S. and Olshan, K. (1970) Evaluative and descriptive aspects in person perception. *J. Personality and Soc. Psychol. 16*, 619-26.

Rosenberg, S. and Sedlak, A. (1972) Structural representations of implicit personality theories, in L. Berkowitz (ed.) *Advances in Experimental Social Psychology, vol. 6.* N.Y.: Academic Press.

Rosenhan, D.L. (1973) On being sane in insane places. *Science 179*, 250-8.

Rosnow, R.L. (1970) Adding and averaging effects in impression formation as a function of the situational context. *Perceptual and Motor Skills 31*, 127-35.

Rosnow, R.L. and Arms, R.L. (1968) Adding versus averaging as a stimulus-combination rule in forming impressions of groups. *J. Personality and Soc. Psychol. 10*, 363-9.

Ross, L., Greene, D. and House, P. (1977) The 'false consensus effect': an egocentric bias in social perception and attribution processes. *J. Exper. Psychol. 13*, 299-301.

Rubin, Z. and Peplau, L.A. (1975) Who believes in a just world? *J. Soc. Issues. 31*, 165-89.

Rugg, H. (1921) Is rating of human character practicable? *J. Educ. Psychol. 12*, 425-38, 485-501.

Russell, B.R. (1927) *Philosophy* N.Y.: Norton.

Ryle, A. and Lunghi, M. (1971) A therapist's prediction of a patient's dyad grid. *Brit. J. Psychiatry 118*, 555-60.

Ryle, G. (1949) *The Concept of Mind.* London: Hutchinson.

Sackett, G.R. (1965) Monkeys reared in isolation with pictures as visual input: evidence for an innate releasing mechanism. *Science 154*, 1468-73.

Sainsbury, P. and Wood, E. (1977) Measuring gesture: its cultural and clinical correlates. *Psycholog. Medicine 7*, 63-72.

Sarbin. T.R., Taft, R., and Bailey, D.E. (1960) *Clinical Inference and Cognitive Theory.* N.Y.: Holt, Rinehart and Winston.

Sawyer, J. (1966) Measurement and prediction, clinical and statistical. *Psycholog. Bull. 66*, 178-200.

Scheflen, A.E. (1965) Quasi-courtship behaviour in psychotherapy. *Psychiatry 28*, 245-57.

Schiffenbauer, A. (1974) Effect of observer's emotional state on judgements of the emotional states of others. *J. Personality and Soc. Psychol. 30*, 31-5.

Schiller, B. (1932) A quantitative analysis of marriage selection in a small group. *J. Soc. Psychol. 3*, 297-319.

Schlosberg, H., (1954) Three dimensions of emotion. *Psycholog. Review 61*, 81-8.

Schneider, D.J. (1973) Implicit personality theory. *Psycholog. Bull. 79*, 294-309.

Schroder, H.E. (1972) Use of feedback in clinical prediction. *J. Consulting and Clin. Psychol. 38*, 265-9.

Scodel, A. and Mussen, P. (1953) Social perceptions of authoritarians and nonauthoritarians. *J. Abnormal and Soc. Psychol. 48*, 181-4.

Sears, R.R. (1936) Experimental studies of projection: 1. Attributions of traits. *J. Soc. Psychol. 7*, 151-63.

Sechrest, L. and Jackson, D.N. (1961) Social intelligence and accuracy of interpersonal predictions. *J. Personality 29*, 167-81.

Secord, P.F. and Backman, C.W. (1964) *Social Psychology*. N.Y.: McGraw-Hill.

Secord, P.F., Bevan, W., Katz, B. (1956) The Negro stereotype and perceptual accentuation. *J. Abnormal and Soc. Psychol. 53*, 78-83.

Shaver, K.G. (1970) Defensive attribution: effects of severity and relevance on the responsibility assigned for an accident. *J. Personality and Soc. Psychol. 14*, 101-13.

Shaw, J. and Skolnick. P. (1971) Attribution of responsibility for a happy accident. *J. Personality and Soc. Psychol. 18*, 380-3.

Shaw, M.E. and Sulzer, J.L. (1964) An empirical test of Heider's levels of attribution of responsibility. *J. Abnormal and Soc. Psychol. 69*, 39-46.

Sherman, M. (1927) The differentiation of emotional responses in infants. *J. Comparative Psychol. 7*, 265-84, 335-51.

Silverman, L.H. (1959) A Q-sort study of the validity of evaluations made from projective tests. *Psycholog. Monographs 73*, no. 7 (Whole no. 477).

Sines, L.K. (1959) The relative contribution for four kinds of data to accuracy in personality assessment. *J. Consulting and Clin. Psychol. 23*, 483-92.

Sisley, E.L. (1970) The breakdown of the American image: comparison of stereotypes held by college students over four decades. *Psycholog. Reports 27*, 779-86.

Slovic, P. (1966) Cue consistency and cue utilization in judgements.

*Am. J. Psychol. 79*, 427-34.

Slovic, P. (1969) Analysing the expert judge: a descriptive study of a stockbroker's decision processes. *J. Applied Psychol. 53*, 255-63.

Smith, H.C. (1966) *Sensitivity to People*. N.Y.: McGraw-Hill.

Snyder, C.R. and Larson, G.R. (1972) A further look at student acceptance of general personality interpretations. *J. Consulting and Clin. Psychol. 38*, 384-8.

Snygg, D. and Coombs, A.W. (1949) *Individual Behaviour: a new frame of reference for psychology*. N.Y.: Harper and Row.

Solomon, D. and Ali, F.A. (1972) Age trends in the perception of verbal reinforcers. *Developmental Psychol. 7*, 238-43.

Spitzer, R.L. and Endicott, J. (1968) Diagno: a computer program for psychiatric diagnosis utilising the Differential Diagnostic Procedure. *Archives of General Psychol. 18*, 746-56.

Spranger, E. (1928) *Types of Men*. Niemeyer.

Stanton, F. and Baker, K.H. (1942) Interviewer bias and the recall of incompletely learned material. *Sociometry 5*, 123-34.

Staw, B.M. (1976) *Intrinsic and Extrinsic Motivation*. Morristown, N.J.: General Learning Press.

Stein, R.T. (1975) Identifying emergent leaders from verbal and non-verbal communications. *J. Personality and Soc. Psychol. 32*, 125-35.

Stein, R.T., Geis, F.L. and Damarin, F. (1973) The perception of emergent leadership in task groups. *J. Personality and Soc. Psychol. 28*, 77-87.

Steiner, I.D. (1955) Interpersonal behaviour as influenced by accuracy of social perception. *Psycholog. Review 62*, 268-74.

Steiner, I.D. and Dodge, J.S. (1957) A comparison of two techniques employed in the study of interpersonal perception. *Sociometry 20*, 1-7.

Storms, M.D. (1973) Videotape and the attribution process: reversing actors' and observers' points of view. *J. Personality and Soc. Psychol. 27*, 165-75.

Storms, M.D. and Nisbett, R.E. (1970) Insomnia and the attribution process. *J. Personality and Soc. Psychol. 16*, 319-28.

Stotland, E. (1969) Exploratory investigations of empathy, in L. Berkowitz (ed.) *Advances in Experimental Social Psychology, vol. 4*. N.Y.: Academic Press.

Stricker, L.J., Jacobs, P.I. and Kogan, N. (1974) Trait interrelations in implicit personality theories and questionnaire data. *J. Personal-*

*ity and Soc. Psychol. 30*, 198-207.

Strongman, K.T. and Hart, C.J. (1968) Stereotyped reactions to body build. *Psycholog. Reports 23*, 1175-8.

Suchman, J.R. (1956) Social sensitivity in the small task-oriented group. *J. Abnormal and Soc. Psychol. 52*, 75-83.

Suedfeld, P. and Rank, A.D. (1976) Revolutionary leaders: long term success as a function of changes in cognitive complexity. *J. Personality and Soc. Psychol. 34*, 169-78.

Taft, R. (1955) The ability to judge people. *Psycholog. Bull. 52*, 1-23.

Taft, R. (1956) Some characteristics of good judges of others. *Brit. J. Psychol. 47*, 19-29.

Tagiuri, R. (1958) Social preference and its perception, in R. Tagiuri and L. Petrullo (eds) *Person Perception and Interpersonal Behaviour*. Stanford Calif.: Stanford University Press.

Taylor, S.E. (1975) On inferring one's attitudes from one's behaviour: some delimiting conditions. *J. Personality and Soc. Psychol. 31*, 126-31.

Taylor. S.E. and Fiske, D.W. (1975) Point of view and perceptions of causality. *J. Personality and Soc. Psychol. 32*, 439-45.

Taylor, S.E. and Koivumaki, J.H. (1976) The perception of self and others: acquaintanceship, affect and actor-observer differences. *J. Personality and Soc. Psychol. 33*, 403-8.

Thibaut, J.W. and Riecken, H.W. (1955) Some determinants and consequences of the perception of social causality. *J. Personality and Soc. Psychol. 32*, 439-45.

Thompson, D.F. and Meltzer, L. (1964) Communication of emotional intent by facial expression. *J. Abnormal and Soc. Psychol. 68*, 129-35.

Thorndike, E. (1918) Fundamental theorems in judging men. *J. Applied Psychol. 2*, 67-76.

Thornton, D.R. (1944) The effect of wearing glasses upon judgements of personality traits of persons seen briefly. *J. Applied Psychol. 28*, 203-7.

Tinbergen, N. (1953) *Social Behaviour in Animals*. London: Methuen.

Toch, H.H., Rabin, A.I. and Wilkins, D.M. (1962) Factors entering into ethnic identifications: an experimental study. *Sociometry 25*, 297-312.

Tomlinson, J.R. (1967) Situational and personality correlates of predictive accuracy. *J. Consulting Psychol. 31*, 19-22.

Trankell, A. (1972) *Reliability of Evidence*. Stockholm: Beckmans.

Tucker, G.R. and Lambert, W.E. (1969) White and Negro listeners' reactions to various American-English dialects. *Social Forces 47*, 463-8.

Tudor, J.F. (1971) The development of class awareness in children. *Social Forces 49*, 470-6.

Udry, J.R. (1963) Complementarity in mate selection: a perceptual approach. *Marriage and family living 25*, 281-9.

Udry, J.R. (1967) Personality match and interpersonal perception as predictors of marriage. *J. Marriage and the Family 29*, 722-5.

Ulrich, L. and Trumbo, D. (1965) The selection interview since 1949. *Psycholog. Bull. 63*, 100-16.

Valentine, C.W. (1929) The relative reliability of men and women in intuitive judgements of character. *Brit. J. Psychol. 19*, 213-88.

Valins, S. (1966) Cognitive effects of false heart rate feedback. *J. Personality and Soc. Psychol. 4*, 400-8.

Valins, S. and Ray, A.A. (1967) Effects of cognitive desensitization of avoidance behaviour. *J. Personality and Soc. Psychol. 7*, 345-50.

Verinis, J.S. and Walker, V., (1970) Policemen and the recall of criminal detail. *J. Soc. Psychol. 81*, 217-21.

Vernon, P.E. (1936) The matching method applied to investigations of personality. *Psycholog. Bull. 33*, 149-77.

Vernon, P.E. (1950) The validation of Civil Service Selection Board procedures. *Occupational Psychol. 25*, 75-95.

Vernon, P.E. (1953) *Personality Tests and Assessments*. London: Methuen.

Vernon, P.E. (1964) *Personality Assessment*. London: Methuen.

Vernon, P.E. and Parry, J.B. (1949) *Personnel Selection in the British Forces*. London: University of London Press.

Walster, E. (1966) Assignment of responsibility for an accident. *J. Personality and Soc. Psychol. 3*, 73-9.

Walster, E. (1967) Second-guessing important events. *Human Relations 20*, 239-50.

Warr, P.B. (1974) Inference magnitude, range and evaluative direction as factors affecting relative importance of cues in impression formation. *J. Personality and Soc. Psychol. 30*, 191-7.

Warr, P.B. and Haycock, V. (1970) Scales for a British personality differential. *Brit. J. Soc. and Clin. Psychol. 9*, 328-37.

Warr, P.B. and Knapper, C. (1968) *The Perception of People and Events*. Chichester: Wiley.

Watson, J.P. (1970) A measure of therapist and patient understanding. *Brit. J. Psychiatry 117*, 319-21.

Webster, E.C. (1964) *Decision-making in the Employment Interview.* Montreal: Industrial Relations Centre, McGill University.

Wedeck, J. (1947) The relationship between personality and 'psychological ability'. *Brit. J. Psychol. 37*, 133-51.

Weiss, H. (1963) Effect of professional training and amount and accuracy of information on behavioural prediction. *J. Consulting Psychol. 27*, 257-62.

Wells, W.D. and Goldstein, R.L. (1964) Sears's study of projection: replications and critique. *J. Soc. Psychol. 64*, 169-79.

Welner, A., Liss, J.L. and Robins, E. (1973) Undiagnosed psychiatric patients: part III, the undiagnosed patient. *Brit. J. Psychiatry 123*, 91-8.

Westcott, M.R. (1968) *Toward a Contemporary Psychology of Intuition.* N.Y.: Holt, Rinehart and Winston.

Weston, M.J. and Whitlock, F.A. (1971) The Capgras syndrome following head injury. *Brit. J. Psychiatry 119*, 25-31.

Wexley, R.N., Yukl, G.A., Kovacs, S.Z. and Sanders, R.E. (1972) Importance of contrast effects in employment interviews. *J. Applied Psychol. 56*, 45-8.

Wiggins, N. and Hoffman, P.J. (1968) Dimensions of profile judgements as a function of instructions, cue-consistency and individual differences. *Multivariate Behavioural Research 3*, 3-20.

Wiggins, N. and Kohen, E.S. (1971) Man versus model of man revisited: the forecasting of graduate school success. *J. Personality and Soc. Psychol. 19*, 100-6.

Wiggins, N., Hoffman, P.J. and Taber, T. (1969) Types of judges and cue utilization in judgements of intelligence. *J. Personality and Soc. Psychol. 12*, 52-9.

Wilkins, E.J. and De Charms, R. (1962) Authoritarianism and response to power cues. *J. Personality 30*, 439-57.

Williams, R.L. and Youssef, Z.I. (1972) Consistency of football coaches in stereotyping the personality of each position's player. *Internat. J. Sports Psychol. 3*, 3-11.

Wing, J.K., Birley, J.LT., Cooper, J.E., Graham, P and Isaacs, A.P. (1967) Reliability of a procedure for measuring and classifying present psychiatric state. *Brit. J. Psychiatry 113*, 499-515.

Wishner, J. (1960) Re-analysis of 'impressions of personality'. *Psycholog. Review 67*, 96-112.

Wolfe, R. (1974) Conceptual level and accuracy of person perception. *Canadian J. Behavioural Science 6*, 309-17.

Wolfson, M.R. and Salancik, G.R. (1977) Observer orientation and actor-observer differences in attributions for failure. *J. Exper. Soc. Psychol. 13*, 441-51.

Woodworth, R.S. (1938) *Experimental Psychology*. N.Y.: Holt, Rinehart and Winston.

Wright, O.R. (1969) Summary of research on the selection interview since 1964. *Personnel Psychol. 22*, 391-413.

Yonge, K.A. (1956) The value of the interview: an orientation and pilot study. *J. Applied Psychol. 40*, 25-31.

Young, R.C. (1972) Clinical judgement as a means of improving actuarial prediction from the MMPI. *J. Consulting and Clin. Psychol. 38*, 457-9.

Zajonc, R. (1960) The process of cognitive tuning in communication. *J. Personality and Soc. Psychol. 61*, 159-67.

Zubin, J. (1967) Classification in the behaviour disorders. *Annual Review of Psychol. 18*, 373-406.

# NAME INDEX

Lawson, E.D., 49
Lay, C.H., 86, 87
Lecompte, W.F., 57
Lee, A.R., 112
Lefebvre, L., 52
Leff, J., 142
Lepper, M.R., 77
Lerner, M.J., 72
Lerner, R.A., 48
Levenson, H., 65
Lewin, A.Y., 139
Ley, P., 142
Liberman, P., 3
Lindgren, H.C., 114
Lindzey, G., 40
Lippman, W., 49
Liss, J.L., 143
Little, B.R., 85, 89
Lopez, L.L., 35
Lowe, C.A., 72
Luchins, A.S., 91
Luginbuhl, J.E.R., 74, 75
Lunghi, M., 113

MacArthur, L.Z., 68
Maccoby, E., 127
Maccoby, N., 131
McCoy, S.A., 142
McHenry, R.E., 51, 65, 104, 105, 107, 115
McIntyre, L.J., 57
McKeachie, W., 49
McKillip, J., 70
Magnusson, D., 36
Magson, E.H., 102, 110, 121
Maier, N.R.F., 53
Mann, J.W., 50
Mannheim, M.D., 39, 106, 116
Maselli, M.D., 70
Matarazzo, J.D., 130
Mayfield, E.C., 136, 141
Meaders, W., 129, 130
Meehl, P.E., 22, 23, 24, 25, 27, 38, 39, 40, 41, 43, 51, 109, 116
Mehrabian, A., 37
Meltzer, L., 122
Milgram, N.A., 130
Milgram, S., 66
Miller, A.G., 66
Miller, D.T., 75
Miller, R.E., 122
Miller, R.L., 79
Miller, W.R., 143

Miron, M.S., 88
Mischel, W., 6, 8, 65, 107, 125, 135
Monson, T.C., 69
Moreno, J.L., 9
Morin, R.E., 20
Mulaik, S.T., 87
Munn, N.L., 108
Munter, P.O., 78
Murphy, G.E., 116
Murray, H.A., 29
Murstein, B.I., 94, 109, 113, 124, 125
Mussen, P., 116, 128

Nicholls, J.G., 75
Nidorf, 86
Nisbett, R.E., 67, 68, 69, 78
Norman, W.T., 87
Notcutt, B., 114
Nystedt, L., 36

Odbert, S., 5, 7, 87
Ogston, D.G., 102
Oldfield, R.C., 6
Olshan, K., 88
O'Neal, E., 90
Osgood, C.E., 37, 82, 86
Oskamp, S., 20, 109, 132

Parry, J.B., 134, 137, 140, 141
Parkinson, C.N., 33, 34, 134, 136
Passini, F.T., 87
Peabody, D., 88
Peplau, L.A., 72
Petersen, D.R., 131
Phillipson, H., 112
Piaget, J., 70, 73
Porter, E.R., 55
Posavac, E.J., 70
Post, D.L., 68
Potkay, C.R., 124
Pritchard, D.A., 42
Pryer, R.S., 94

Raabe, V.L., 128
Rabin, A.I., 105
Rabinowitz, N., 117
Ramsey, G.V., 81
Ray, A.A., 78
Raymond, B.J., 48
Reid, T., 16
Remmers, H.H., 113
Richards, J.M., 112, 126
Riecken, H.W., 60

# SUBJECT INDEX